This publication is made possible by the generous support of:
Akvafifth Club, *Chicago, Illinois*
Jerald & Ricke Bly in memory of Harald Hakon Madsen, *Tyler, Minnesota*
Bygghouse LLC, *Merchantville, New Jersey*
Dania Society of Chicago
Chuck & Joanne Frederiksen, *Ames, Iowa*
Bill & Joann Jensen, *Urbandale, Iowa*
Craig & Shannon Jensen, *Audubon, Iowa*
Steve Jensen
Rebild National Park Society, Inc.
Gwynn & Chuck Siemen, *Lexington, Kentucky*
And 198 additional supporters who contributed to the Kickstarter campaign for this publication

This publication is created in conjunction with the exhibition
***Skål! Scandinavian Spirits* presented by Aalborg and Linie aquavits.**

Additional exhibition sponsors include:
Albert V. Ravenholt Fund, *Seattle, Washington*
American Swedish Historical Museum, *Philadelphia, Pennsylvania*
American-Scandinavian Foundation, *New York, New York*

***Skål! Scandinavian Spirits* was organized by the Museum of Danish America in Elk Horn, Iowa**

In cooperation with the following partner venues:
Nordic Heritage Museum, *Seattle, Washington*
Swedish American Museum, *Chicago, Illinois*
Vesterheim Norwegian-American, Museum *Decorah, Iowa*
American Swedish Historical Museum, *Philadelphia, Pennsylvania*
American Swedish Institute, *Minneapolis, Minnesota*

ISBN 978-0-692-41388-3

www.danishmuseum.org

Edited by Tova Brandt, Albert Ravenholt Curator of Danish-American Culture, *Museum of Danish America*

Book design by Oxide Design Co., *Omaha, Nebraska*

Skål!
Scandinavian
Spirits

presented by
Aalborg and Linie Aquavits

Organized by the
Museum of Danish America
Elk Horn, Iowa

Table of contents

Letter from Arcus AS,
manufacturer of Aalborg and Linie aquavits

Dear Reader,

Skål! Arcus, the company that makes Aalborg and Linie aquavit, is proud to be the presenting sponsor of the Skål! Scandinavian Spirits travelling exhibition. Arcus is a company of dedicated spirits enthusiasts who truly cherish the complexity and diversity that our Scandinavian spirits have to offer. We are thankful for this opportunity to share with you our joy and passion for this vital part of Scandinavian heritage and traditional culture.

Aquavits are at the very heart of our business. The knowledge of how to produce these timeless tokens of Scandinavian identity has literally been passed on from generation to generation for hundreds of years. The first mention of aquavit ever recorded is from the year 1531, when Archbishop of Nidaros (today Trondheim) Olav Engelbrektsson received a noble gift called "Aqua vit", meaning "water of life", as a form of medicine that was then believed to cure "all illness any man could carry inside". He loved it!

A lot has of course changed since then, but the people's love for aquavit has just grown stronger. Today, Arcus manufactures and sells millions of liters of aquavit in several countries across Europe and North America. In Scandinavia, we currently supply some 50 different quality brands including the famous Aalborg aquavit and Lysholm Linie aquavit, which you can read more about inside of this publication, along with a broad range of other premium aquavit brands such as Gammel Opland aquavit, Gilde aquavit and Løiten aquavit.

Aquavit should be enjoyed. Either as a compliment with food, or as an ingredient for drinks and cocktails. Yes, aquavit actually makes terrific drinks! We believe our spirits can enrichen meals, provide great alternatives for making drinks, and help create the special moments in life when you really feel you are enjoying yourself! We believe in social companionship and enjoyment together with the people you love. And we believe in responsible drinking.

That being said, we wish you a pleasant journey of discovery through the world of Scandinavian spirits! On behalf of some 250 dedicated craftsmen, distillers, developers, operators, salesmen, managers and other Arcus personnel, Skål!

Your Arcus Team and

Christer A. Olsen,
Arcus Business Area Manager USA

Skål – The Spirit of Scandinavia

By John Mark Nielsen,
Executive Director,
Museum of Danish America

Bright eyes and expectant faces across a candle lit table. Porcelain dishes and gleaming glasses, large and small. Aromas of pickled herring, spiced meats, aged cheeses and aromatic condiments. The scent of fried fish fillets, roasting meats and steamed vegetables. The anticipation of good food and spirited conversation.

The pickled herring and dark, full-grain rye bread is served. The schnapps glasses are filled; the bottles of beer or sparkling water are opened. The host and hostess raise their glasses and, looking each guest in the eye, speak the time honored words: "Skål og velkommen!"

How does a museum present the ephemeral aspects of a culture? Food and drink, and the ritual ways they are presented and consumed reveal important social and cultural values. This is certainly true of the beer and aquavit of the Scandinavian countries. How too does a museum acknowledge the suffering and sorrow that in this case abuse of alcohol can cause?

I have experienced the richness of the tradition. I had my first beer on a family farm on the Danish island of Fyn when I was thirteen. My great aunt had brewed the beer we drank. In fact brewing ale was an important role of Scandinavian housewives dating back long before the Viking era. I remember it being dark, with a frothy head, and it was sweet, almost like root beer. I had never had anything like it and later suffered from slight over indulgence!

A week later, we were in Herning, visiting the family of my great uncle Johann. We started lunch with rye bread and pickled herring. I remember "Onkel Johann" pouring a small amount of Aalborg Akvavit in to a schnapps glass and saying with a smile, "Now that you are confirmed, you are an adult. It's time that you learn to drink aquavit. Skål!" (I suspect his smile was in anticipation of my response to the ice cold, clear liquid.) I remember it burned, but it worked with herring, and after all, as he said, "the fish needed something to swim in."

But I also learned from an early age that drunkenness was a sin. In particular, I remember a Sunday school lesson from the Book of Genesis about Noah's drunkenness and nakedness. After the flood, he and his three sons had planted grapes, made wine, and Noah had drunk too much. This led to family discord and break-up.

My father was a pastor in what was the United Danish Evangelical Lutheran Church, a church where some members where deeply influenced by the Inner Mission, a pietistic movement in Denmark that believed consumption of alcohol was a sin. In both Scandinavia and among Scandinavian-Americans there were those who shared this position, and it led to prohibition movements in all Scandinavian countries and support for prohibition in this country.

Over the years, I have participated in many a "Danish" dinner party, both in Denmark and here in the United States. I have always appreciated them for the food and good conversation, and of course the beer and the aquavit! Such gatherings have inspired profound feelings of gratitude to join with family and friends around the table.

The exhibit, Skål – Scandinavian Spirits, focuses on the history and artifacts surrounding the brewing of beer and the distilling of aquavit in Scandinavia. As you learn the stories and see the exhibited artifacts, I invite you to reflect on the ways these are indicators of Scandinavian culture, both positive and negative. I also hope that you will remember events when you have raised your glass and, catching the eye of surrounding guests, said, maybe even shouted: "Skål!"

We at the Museum of Danish America would not have been able to create this exhibit without the support of many. I especially want to thank Arcus AS of Norway for their being the major corporate sponsor of this exhibit. I also want to thank the Albert V. Ravenholt Fund and the American-Scandinavian Foundation for their support. Finally, I also want to acknowledge and thank the directors and curators of the Nordic Heritage Museum in Seattle, the American Swedish Institute in Minneapolis, the Swedish American Museum in Chicago, the American Swedish Historical Museum in Philadelphia, and Vesterheim Norwegian-American Museum in Decorah, Iowa. This has been the first collaborative effort by all the major Scandinavian-American museums; it is as if we all have gathered around the table – "Skål!"

Three men in the Danish Village of Kimballton, Iowa, share good spirits at the Andersen photo studio.
Museum of Danish America

SECTION 2

A Spirited Heritage

By Tova Brandt, Albert Ravenholt Curator of Danish-American Culture, *Museum of Danish America*

Raise your glass.

Look your companions in the eye.

Say "Skål!" with gusto.
(pronounced "skoal")

Take a drink.

Look your companions in the eye again.

Set down your glass.

For many Scandinavian Americans, this ritual is an expression of their heritage. What's in the glass? If the contents match the custom, then it's probably either beer or aquavit.

The word "Skål" itself has origins made misty over time. Some claim that the term has a root in the skulls of the vanquished, from which Viking warriors would drink to celebrate their victory. But this is a grisly story, and most likely just a story. In more recent times, wooden bowls – sometimes elaborately decorated – would be filled with beer and passed from person to person at community gatherings like weddings or festival days. The word for bowl is "skål" in Danish, Swedish and Norwegian. From that tradition of passing the bowl, the term "Skål" is now also a toast – "Cheers!"

Just as certain cookies are part of Scandinavian Christmas traditions, so are traditional beverages often found where celebration and ethnic heritage intersect. An open-faced sandwich of pickled herring, a shot of dill-flavored aquavit, and a bottle of Carlsberg beer – for some Danish Americans, they could hardly have one without the other. Though Scandinavian-Americans may seek out beverages from their own homelands – Norway, Denmark or Sweden – the cultural history and traditions are shared throughout Scandinavia.

Definitions

Øl *(in Danish and Norwegian)*
Öl *(in Swedish)*

Beer or ale.

Brændevin *(in Danish)*
Brännvin *(in Swedish)*
Brennevin *(in Norwegian)*

The term for distilled liquor – usually what we would call vodka today. Literally the term translates to "burnt wine" which refers to the early history of distilling in Scandinavia when wine was used as a raw material. Brændevin is sometimes translated as "brandy", but in Scandinavian history the terms applies to distilled liquor from grain, and later from potatoes. In the early period of distilling, the results often tasted awful – this led to adding herbs and other plants to improve the flavor, creating what we now know as aquavit.

Aquavit *(akvavit in Danish and Swedish)*
Akevitt *(in Norwegian)*

A specific term for vodka flavored with caraway and other herbs and spices. Literally, the term comes from the Latin aqua vitae, the water of life.

Snaps

A more general term for flavored liquor – it could be caraway-flavored aquavit, or it could feature different ingredients. Using the term "snaps" is more common in Denmark than in Norway or Sweden.

Top to bottom:
Tuborg Beer Coaster,
Swedish American Line Coaster,
Tuborg Beer Coaster.
Museum of Danish America

Poster commercial for Taffel Aquavit. De Danske Spritfabrikker (The Danish Spirit Factories).
Courtesy of Arcus AS

Distinctively Danish

AALBORG AKVAVIT

With buffet supper, canapes or sn
gasbord, the right spirit makes
occasion. Aalborg Akvavit, served
cold and straight, is smooth, dry
delicious — delightfully different.

Sole Distr. U.S.A. Munson G. Shaw
N. Y. 86 proof, 100% grain neutral sp

Carlsberg poster, 1905.
From the Carlsberg Image Gallery

Aalborg Akvavit advertised in the
Svenska Posten, 1967.
Nordic Heritage Museum

Wassail bowl. Wood and paint, circa 1850, Sweden.
American Swedish Heritage Museum

From Egil's Saga *(c.1230)*

Egil and his men are engaged in a drinking contest with their host, Armod:

"One man was given the job of serving each toast to Egil and his men, and kept egging them on to drink up quickly, but Egil told his men not to have any more, and he drank their share, that being the only way out of it. When Egil realized that he couldn't keep going any longer, he stood up, walked across the floor to Armod, put both hands on his shoulders and pressed him up against the pillar, then heaved up a vomit of massive proportions that gushed all over Armod's face…"

(translation by Hermann Pálsson and Paul Edwards, 1976)

A Spirited History

Scandinavians have brewed beer for over 1500 years. In pre-Christian times, the Norse god Odin was credited with teaching humans how to brew beer, and drinking beer was often involved in worship and as offering to the deities. The Norse sagas mention drinking beer, especially in celebration of battle victories, and sometimes in the form of drinking challenges. When harvests were small, beer brewing was restricted to special occasions in order to reserve enough grain for food preparation.

Through the Middle Ages and up to the 19th century, beer remained an important part of daily life and festive traditions. As in much of northern Europe, beer was a common beverage for everyone in society – men, women and children. Beer provided more sustenance and was usually safer to drink than local water sources, which were often contaminated. The alcohol content was likely around 2%, much lower than most beers made today.

For special events, brewing and consuming beer followed long-established traditions. In Norway, wedding preparations might include brewing 10 to 12 barrels of ale to share with guests over many days. Similar brewing traditions marked Easter, Pentecost, and other life events like harvests or funerals. Decorative ale bowls reinforced the festive nature of the celebration; passing those bowls from person to person reinforced the social ties within the community.

Inscriptions painted in ale bowls include:

 Drink my friend, pass it to your neighbor then.

 A little drink is good for a man, but if he wants more, take the bowl away from him.

 A bowl of beer on the farmer's table is better than many sweet words.

Drinking bowls and drinking horns are some of the details of daily life visible in the Bayeux Tapestry, which depicts the story of William of Normandy conquering England in 1066. Both William and the defeated Harold were direct descendants of the Viking migrations of the prior two centuries.

Delivery wagons loaded up at the Carlsberg beer factory in Copenhagen, Denmark, early 20th century.
Museum of Danish America

The Great Nordic Intoxication

In the 1500s *brændevin* (distilled liquor) became known through Scandinavia, initially distributed as a medical cure-all. But more extensive – and disruptive – use was clearly becoming common by 1551 when King Christian III of Denmark and Norway banned the serving of *brændevin* on holidays in an attempt to prevent people attending church while drunk. Two generations later, Christian IV ordered the parliament to meet at 7am so that members weren't too intoxicated to conduct business. Between the growing production of *brændevin* and the regular consumption of beer, this period has been called "The Great Nordic Intoxication" by several historians. Even livestock became tipsy when fed the fermented by-products of alcohol production.

"I will probably rather have a glass of *brændevin*, as it is too early to drink beer."

From the comedy by Ludvig Holberg, Erasmus Montanus, 1723

By the 1600s, *brændevin* was widely available through home-based distilling in Denmark and Sweden; the results often tasted awful and therefore required additional ingredients to mask the taste – thus, caraway-flavored aquavit was born. Taxes on *brændevin* and the copper kettles used in distilling started to appear in the 1600s, as did attempts by the State to restrict distilleries to towns. Illegal distilling continued, however, and by the mid-1700s nearly half of Danish families were able to distill their own *brændevin* – a legacy that is still evident in the Danish root word for brewing (*brygge*) found in the name of what Americans would call the utility room in the home (*bryggers*).

Starting in the 1800s, Scandinavian governments grew more successful at controlling the production and sale of alcohol. Industrialization led to a better product, and also to larger businesses taking the lion's share of the alcohol trade. Through the 19th century and into the early 20th the numbers of distilleries and breweries continued to shrink.

Tuborg beer wagon, 1917.
Photo courtesy of Robert Rasmussen

Tuborg beer van, 1956.
Photo courtesy of Robert Rasmussen

KLÆDEDRAGTER I KIØBENHAVN.
En Brændeviinsmand. — Ein Brandweinsbrenner.

"Brændeviinsmand" engraving by Johannes Senn,
early 1800s.
*Used with permission from the
Copenhagen City Museum*

Norway had about 11,000 home stills in the 1820s, which dropped to 450 in the 1850s. Sweden saw a similar dramatic drop from 33,000 to 500 home stills. Denmark had 2500 legal distilleries in 1800, which dropped to 52 in 1900.

Why the decline in home production?

- Increased taxes on distillation equipment.

- Preference for using potatoes (rather than grain) as the source for distilling aquavit, which required more sophisticated equipment and a larger scale of production.

- Laws prohibiting home production.

Founded in the 19th century, continuing in the 21st.

Many of the companies that dominate Scandinavian beer and aquavit production today were founded in this period of greater industrialization:

- **Carlsberg beer** *(Denmark, 1847)*

- **Tuborg beer** *(Denmark, 1873)*

- **Ringnes beer** *(Norway, 1876)*

- **Hansa beer** *(Norway, 1882)*

- **De Danske Spritfabrikker (The Danish Spirits factories, DDSF)** *(Denmark, 1881)*
  DDSF named their aquavit Aalborg in honor of their founders' home city. By 1923, DDSF had bought out all other distilleries in Denmark and had a monopoly on aquavit production.

- **Absolut Rent Brännvin** *(Sweden, 1879)*
  In Sweden, the "vodka king," Lars Olsson Smith (1836-1913), started producing Absolut Rent Brännvin in 1879 – not to be confused with Absolut Vodka, which would become one of Sweden's most successful exports in the 1980s.

Migration of Drinking Traditions

Large waves of Scandinavian immigrants arrived in the United States beginning in the middle of the 19th century and reaching a peak in the years around 1900.

"I should have brewed some beer for Christmas, all preparations were made, but a keg is very difficult to get hold of here. We had finally been promised one from a man, but when this same man wanted a christening a couple of months after Munch had conducted his marriage and was accosted for this, he got angry, and we lost the keg. I had been afraid this would happen, and I asked Munch to consider that we were to borrow this keg, but he would not even listen to me, although he dearly wanted that beer. Thus we had trouble for our pains instead of Christmas brew."

Caja Munch, a pastor's wife and Norwegian immigrant, writing in January 1857

As Scandinavians started new lives in America, some traditions remained and some did not. Many immigrants in the 19th century continued to brew beer for weddings and other uses. In some Norwegian-American communities in North Dakota, large weddings still included alcohol provided by the hosts, even after the state became dry in 1890. Home-based distilling, though, had largely declined in Scandinavia by the time mass emigration began and did not continue as a common tradition in the United States. Many immigrants frequented taverns or saloons for a drink with neighbors or co-workers; these taverns were largely the domain of working men, and shifted the balance of alcohol and community that had been part of Scandinavian tradition.

Advertisements for imported aquavit *(brændevin)* in Scandinavian-American newspapers *Bien* (The Bee), California, 1903, 1956, and 1934.

Museum of Danish America, Digital Library of Danish-American Newspapers

Men, women and children harvesting hops,
circa 1900.
Nordic Heritage Museum

The Bridge Way Tavern offered meals and a
variety of beer in Ballard, the Scandinavian
neighborhood of Seattle. For some temperance
supporters, promoting beer was a strategy to
moderate alcohol consumption.
Nordic Heritage Museum

Meeting of the International Order of the Good Templars, Seattle, Washington.
Nordic Heritage Museum

IOGT

The International Order of Good Templars (IOGT) is one temperance organization with a long history among Scandinavian Americans. Lodges of the IOGT served as social halls and hosted a wide variety of events, all in an alcohol-free environment. Groups like the IOGT offered alternative gathering spaces and social networks for Scandinavian Americans.

"It's Okay Not to Drink"

Temperance movements were on the rise throughout Scandinavia in the 19th and early 20th centuries. Increasing alcohol abuse prompted some reformers to seek moderating strategies, such as promoting beer as an alternative to strong liquor. Religious revivals inspired pietists to call for an end to drinking, as well as dancing, card games, and other perceived sources of temptation; many Scandinavian immigrants to the United States were pietists and carried their convictions with them to America.

Through the early 20th century, Norway, Sweden and Denmark each developed different ways to exert state control over production and consumption. Norway banned production and importation of alcohol from 1919 to 1926; after repealing the ban, all sales were required to go through the *Vinmonopol* (Wine Monopoly). Sweden rationed alcohol from 1919 to 1955 and limited all sales to state-controlled stores. Denmark imposed a high alcohol tax in 1917 which was unpopular, but probably avoided a system of state control or outright prohibition.

In the United States, the National Prohibition Act of 1919 – informally known as the Volstead Act – became the law of the land in 1920. It was named for the U.S. Representative who introduced the legislation, Andrew John Volstead, a Norwegian-American born in Kenyon, Minnesota, and a graduate of St. Olaf College. Most conservative Scandinavian Americans were great supporters of Prohibition. They saw alcohol as a social evil, often an outright sin, and thus saw it as their Christian duty to completely rid society of it – by law if needed. More liberal communities opposed the prohibitive approach; they recognized drunkenness was a problem, but they thought Prohibition limited personal freedom and simply didn't work.

Meeting of the International Order of the Good
Templars, Seattle, Washington.
Nordic Heritage Museum

National Total Abstinence Federation
Annual Meeting, 1911.
Vesterheim Norwegian-American Museum

"Announcement to the Norwegian and Danish
People in America, from the Scandinavian Society
for the Total Abstinence in Minnesota"

Program announcement for a temperance society,
Minneapolis, 1887.
Vesterheim Norwegian-American Museum

Tuborg coasters.
Museum of Danish America

"Norwegian Sweater Day" at the Torske Klub of
Chicago in January 2015. The cod mounted inside
the glass case is the namesake for the club (the
torsk) and attends every meeting.
Photo courtesy of the Chicago Torske Klub

Scandinavian Spirits

Scandinavian drinking traditions offer one way for Scandinavian Americans to connect to their heritage within families, social groups, or ethnic institutions. Even in the early 20th century, Scandinavian-American groups included aquavit in their event menus – and apologized if it wasn't there! Increasing global trade through the 20th century provided regular access to imported beer and aquavit from Scandinavia, allowing Americans to seek out these beverages directly from their ancestral homelands. The dominant breweries and distilleries in Scandinavia sought export markets for their products, and marketed them accordingly.

More recently, American companies have started to produce Scandinavian-style aquavit. Gamle Ode was founded in Minnesota, inspired by Danish hospitality traditions, and engaged members of the Danish American Center in Minneapolis as taste-testers when the founders experimented with recipes. Opened in 2013, the Old Ballard Liquor Company in Seattle creates spirits – including a seasonal selection of aquavit and snaps – that celebrate the blue-collar Scandinavian heritage of the Ballard neighborhood. House Spirits Distillery, founded in 2004 in Portland, Oregon, features two flavors of their Krogstad Aquavit, as well as Volstead Vodka named in honor of the Norwegian-American sponsor of Prohibition.

After Prohibition was repealed in 1933, heritage organizations could again officially include alcohol in their programs. For example, several Torske klub groups (literally "Cod Clubs") were established in Norwegian-American communities like Minneapolis (1933), Chicago (1960), and Madison, Wisconsin (1977); these groups of Norwegian-American men still gather regularly to share a meal of cod, potatoes, and aquavit. Similarly, Danish-American members the Akvafifth Club in Chicago have met monthly since 1982 to celebrate their shared appreciation of aquavit; they marked their 10th and 25th anniversary years with tours of Denmark and Danish distilleries.

Assorted aquavits, domestic and imported.
Photos by Kimberly Ann Newman and Mike McCarron

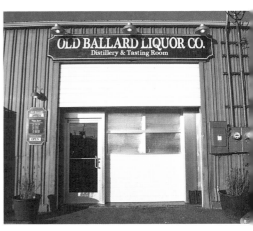

Old Ballard Liquor Co., Seattle, Washington.
Photo by Jill Rachel Evans

Carlsberg poster, 1958.
From the Carlsberg Image Gallery

Carlsberg beer.
Museum of Danish America

Julefrokost (Christmas Lunch)

This satirical drawing shows a stereotypical Danish family gathering for *Julefrokost*. While the tradition remains as a family Christmas meal, *Julefrokost* is now also a festive event to be shared with colleagues and friends. Depending on the circumstances, a *Julefrokost* might involve loads of food, heavy drinking, and a fair share of embarrassing moments.

By Peter Hermann, www.phermann.com

Holidays provide another connection between heritage and celebration.

Christmas / Jul

December and January are filled with celebrations of good food, good drink, and good company. In Scandinavia today, a popular part of the season is the Julebord or Julfrokost, a holiday party shared with co-workers, friends, families, or other groups. One might attend several events through the holidays, all accompanied with Christmas beers and aquavit. (In Norway, half of all aquavit sold is consumed around Christmas.) Another traditional Christmas beverage in both Scandinavian and Scandinavian-American homes is glögg – a warm, spiced wine or punch.

Midsummer

The longest day of the year has always been reason to celebrate in Scandinavia, as the contrast with short winter days is so dramatic. Celebrated with bonfires, music, and a picnic atmosphere, midsummer is a perfect opportunity to share a "skål" with friends and neighbors.

Crayfish Parties

This Swedish tradition celebrates the traditional opening of the crayfish season in August. The fish need "something to swim in," therefore beer and aquavit are in ample supply.

Christmas lunch at Restaurant Kronborg.
Photo by Thomas Alcayaga. www.madetmere.dk.
Copenhagen

P.S. Krøyer, "Midsummer Eve bonfire on Skagen's beach," 1906.
Skagen Museum

Midsummer (Sankt Hans Aften)
Decorah, Iowa, 2014.
Photograph by Charlie Langton

A sampling of open-faced sandwiches.
Restaurant Kronborg, www.restaurantkronborg.dk.
Photo by Martin Kaufmann

Danish-Americans enjoying some
home-infused snaps.
Museum of Danish America

Do you have to have Scandinavian DNA to enjoy the traditions of Scandinavian drinking? No, of course not!

The Do-It-Yourselfer

Try flavoring your own aquavit or snaps! No special equipment required, just a bottle of vodka and some jars to infuse the flavorings of your choice.

The Foodie

Explore varied pairings of pickled herring with chilled aquavit. Or open-faced sandwiches, or holiday meals, or …

The Modern Viking

Leave your swords at the door and share the beverage of your choice in fellowship with your neighbors. Communal vessel optional.

The Designer

Stylish drinkware is just as important as the contents: enjoy the experience for the eyes, the hands, and the tastebuds.

The Genealogist

Learn more about what your ancestors drank. Keep the tradition alive!

The Mixologist

Try a favorite cocktail with a Scandinavian twist, or create something entirely new!

From the fire-lit halls of the Vikings to the micro-distilleries of today, Scandinavian traditions of beer and aquavit offer many ways to celebrate with friends and family. As the verse on one Norwegian ale bowl says, "Drink my friend, pass it to your neighbor then." Gather your friends, raise your glass, and share a "Skål!"

Midsummer (*Sankt Hans Aften*)
Decorah, Iowa, 2014.
Photograph by Charlie Langton.

Midsummer (*Sankt Hans Aften*)
Decorah, Iowa, 2014.
Photo by Jane Kemp

Festive Events and Ale Drinking in Traditional Norway

By Carol Hasvold, former Registrar and Librarian,
Vesterheim Norwegian-American Museum

Acanthus-carved beaker, Gudbrandsdal, Norway,
ca. 1890-1900.
Vesterheim Norwegian-American Museum

It is a huge challenge for persons in the 21st century to try to imagine how people in rural Norway lived two centuries ago. Fortunately, modern Norwegian scholars have been engaged in this endeavor also. From early sources they interpret the complex relationships, social patterns and mores that gave rural communities their shape. They utilize such primary sources as H.J. Wille's description of the Seljord parish in Telemark, written in 1786, which describes both economic and social life in the eighteenth century. Another important source is M.B. Landstad's description of people and folkways that he encountered in his early days (1840s and 50s) as a young itinerant pastor in Telemark and other regions of Norway. Modern writers draw on these and rich unpublished material in Norwegian archival collections as well. With their help we attempt to jump backward in time and peer into the lives and traditions of 19th-century Norwegians.

Ale bowl with rosemaling, Telemark, Norway,
ca. 1850.
Vesterheim Norwegian-American Museum

Ale bowl with rosemaling, Telemark, Norway,
1807 or 1867.
Vesterheim Norwegian-American Museum

Ale bowl with decorative painting, Norway, 1751.
Vesterheim Norwegian-American Museum

Inscription: *Drik hvis at det dig
behager. Lad den ingen gaa forbi -
send mig bollen tom tilbage, fylde den
igjen jeg vil.*

Translation: *Drink if it pleases you.
Don't let it pass by. Send my bowl back
to me empty and I will fill it again.*

Ale drinking in Norway had its background in pre-Christian times. Ancient
worship often took the form of a "blote," drinking as an offering to God,
a way to draw near to God. In the 11th century, when Christianity was
established in Norway, drinking and brewing of ale were limited to a few
special times of the year.

Society changed through the centuries, but up through the time when
the Norwegians began immigrating to America, there was still much
influence from olden times. Most Norwegians coming to the United
States in the 19th century were of peasant background, so much of what
is described here still applied to many families in emigration times.

Festive celebrations were part of the country culture. There were two kinds
of festive events: those linked to certain times of the year, such as Christmas
and harvest time; and those related to life events, such as marriage or death.
Drinking ale, passing lavishly decorated bowls of home brew from person to
person, was an honored part of celebrating all significant events in Norwegian
traditional culture. In these special events the people made the connection
between the everyday and the sacred. In the way the events were carried out,
the individual reinforced his place within society; in ritualized behavior,
everyone had their place and fulfilled their role.

Wooden tap, Norway, 1830-1870.
Vesterheim Norwegian-American Museum

Inscription: *För stod jeg I den grönne Lund, og ingen mig mone kjende, nu mætter jeg mangen törstig Mund*

Translation: *Previously I was standing in the green grove (of trees), and no one might know me, now I satisfy many a thirsty mouth.*

Brewing and Serving

An important part of the preparation for a festive event was the brewing of the ale. In the early 19th century, 10-12 barrels of ale might be brewed for a wedding, or 4-6 barrels for a lesser event. Neighbors contributed food or money to the events, which could be expensive, as they were community events.

Sprouted and dried barley was ground, cooked and fermented according to recipes handed down through many generations, all the way from the Norse god Odin, who first taught brewing to humans. But the important thing was that the ale be strong and good. Strong ale was a sign that the farm was prosperous and well managed.

There was a connection between strong ale and fire, strength and virility. It helped to have a vigorous fire under the cooking pot, and if possible some young men should fight and wrestle around the room. Also it was very unlucky to sweep the floor when brewing was going on: "the dirtier the floor, the better the ale will be," was the saying.

Horse-handled ale bowl, Norway, 1829.
Vesterheim Norwegian-American Museum

Ale goose, Norway, 1830-1870.
Vesterheim Norwegian-American Museum

In medieval times the most common vessel for drinking ale was the horn of an ox or goat. These curved horns were used for ceremonial occasions as late as the 19th century, and were often decorated with bands or feet of silver. Turned wooden bowls exist from the fifteenth century on, at first plain, and after 1700 painted with colorful floral designs and also with inscriptions as well. Many inscriptions encourage the drinker to enjoy the øl, but also to drink moderately and pass the bowl on to the next person. This was communal drinking; bowls larger than 7" diameter were passed from hand to hand. Richly painted bowls, pouring tankards and carved bowls with handles in the shapes of animal or human figures reflect the tradition of ale drinking at festive occasions.

Ram-head handled ale bowl, Norway.
Vesterheim Norwegian-American Museum

Inscription: *Drik lystikt mi venn. Mor tapper ijen*

Translation: *Drink merrily, my friend. Mother is tapping again.*

Christmas Traditions

The brewing of the ale for Christmas would take place in early December. Dippers of the ale could be tapped out from the barrels on December 21, to see that the ale was working well. This was Thomas the Brewer's Day, which was an observance significant enough to be marked on the medieval calendar sticks. This was a day when neighbors went from house to house, sampling the new ale, or "tilting the bowl."

Everyone had a special role at Christmas. The father gave the animals extra feed and set up the kornband, a sheaf of grain put on the peak of a roof, so even the birds were well fed. He also would paint crosses with tar or pitch on doorposts of the out-buildings to fend off evil spirits which might be roaming the countryside.

Mother cleaned the house and put straw on the floor, on which the family would sleep, leaving the beds for the ancestors whose spirits might come back and pay a visit in the Christmas season. She prepared especially rich food such as pork and lefse and rømmegrøt. A bowl of rømmegrøt also had to be set out for the julenisse. If this little Christmas elf was not well treated, he would see to it that the cows would not give any milk and the horses would go lame! Everyone had a bath and put on clean clothes, to be prepared for the coming of the Christ Child.

On Christmas Eve, the father received the family and also other workers on the farm in front of the big fireplace in the stue, the main room of the house, wished them all Merry Christmas, and poured ale from a spouted stave pitcher (kanne) into the waiting bowls so everyone felt warmed and welcomed and full of Christmas gladness. On this evening, the ale flowed generously, and all were treated graciously, from the farmer's sons and daughters, to the tenant farmers and milkmaids.

Late in the evening, when all had eaten and drunk their fill, the father would go out and fire a gun into the air, and the halloos echoed down from one country valley to the next. There was a saying, "You can hear that people have something to make themselves happy with!"

On Christmas Day, Første Juledag, it was the custom for all to go to church, and the Prest (priest) often had a real challenge to keep the crowd quiet and orderly for the Christmas Gospel and sermon! Landstad was especially concerned about drinking of hard liquor when it was available in the countryside. He felt that ale was part of the celebration but that aquavit was an abuse.

Valdres House, built in Valdres, Norway in 1795 and relocated to Decorah, Iowa in 1976.
Vesterheim Norwegian-American Museum

Inscription: *Driker du mere en du eter Kan du lige der du siter.*

Translation: *If you drink more than you eat you can lie where you are sitting.*

In olden times, when the sun was at its lowest ebb on December 21, people believed that the sun had died. By Tredje Juledag, the third day of Christmas, it was apparent that the days were growing longer, so this day was also very festive. A man might sit on the floor with a bowl of ale between his knees, pick up the bowl with his mouth only and drink it down. Then again with his mouth only, he would toss the bowl over his shoulder. If the bowl landed upside down, there was a good chance he would die or have another kind of disaster in the year to come. If it landed right-side up, he would live to drink the Christmas ale again!

Easter and Pentecost were also events for brewing ale, but to a lesser extent. On Langfredag, Good Friday, they baked ash cakes, reflecting a more religious character to the Easter season than was the case at Christmas, which was tied to the death and revival of the sun.

There were other occasions for minor celebrations and thus for brewing and passing around the ale bowl. This could be at Sanct Hans Dag (June 23), at harvest, for bringing the cows down from the mountain pastures, and on other occasions when farmers or families may have worked together. In the 18th century rural Norway there was a custom called a kast, or throw. If a family was very poor, they could invite their neighbors to a dance. People would donate food and ale, come and dance and drink, and "kast" food, clothing, or household goods in a pile for the aid of the impoverished family.

Spouted ale pitcher, Norway, 1750.
Vesterheim Norwegian-American Museum,
Luther College Collection

Inscription: *Naar alt er vaek de mig*
for glemmer. Naar jeg er met. Na har
jeg kenner.

Translation: *When everything is gone*
they forget me. When I am full, now I
have friends.

Wedding Traditions

A great event for brewing which was not tied to the time of year was a wedding. After a year or two of courtship and exchange of sweetheart gifts, a match was agreed upon. The young man and his friends built up their courage by playing the fiddle, dancing and drinking lots of ale. They then processed on horseback to the bride's home, carrying a large bowl of ale, showing their support for the groom. The bride's mother and aunties were helping her to dress in festive costume, including possibly a silver or gold crown which had been passed down for generations in her family.

The groom and groomsmen negotiated with the bride's father, with much passing of the ale bowl back and forth. The fiddler played more music, the bride came down and there was more dancing and passing of the ale bowl. When the bride price was settled, hundre daler, hest og sadel (hundred dollars, horse and saddle) was the saying, all drank three big skåls to seal the bargain.

The bridal price settled, with much music and passing of the ale bowl, the bridal procession wended its way through the valleys and perhaps even over the fjord to church. The Prest had to keep order and accomplish the union properly, as he represented both the church and the civil authorities. A nineteenth century painting shows the Prest meeting the group at the church with a silver ale tankard in his hand, showing that drinking of ale was understood to be part of the event.

The wedding party then went to the home where the couple would reside, and the music, feasting, and drinking of ale continued for at least two or three days. In some areas, when the party was coming to its end, people drained their bowls and tossed silver coins in, both as gifts and as a help to defray the cost of the celebration.

Silver tankard, Norway, 1752.
Vesterheim Norwegian-American Museum,
Luther College Collection

Funeral Traditions

The third big time for feasting and drinking was the burial of the dead. This was not exactly a time of celebration, but a time to get the dead properly buried and to show social support for the family. The dying person often supervised the building of his own coffin as well as the brewing of the gravøl, the funeral ale.

When the person died, or "let go," as the saying was, the neighbors were invited to the house, and each came with a gift of food or ale. The casket sat on a table covered with a white cloth, surrounded by cross and candles. Mourners came in, made the sign of the cross over the casket and prayed the Lord's Prayer. When all were assembled, the people stood in a ring around the casket, and it was opened for a final viewing. The assembled company sang three hymns, with long pauses between the verses for the passing of ale. The lid was fixed on the casket, which was then carried to the door. A family member spoke on behalf of the deceased, in appreciation for the friendship and support which had been enjoyed in the past. This was the "parting toast." The casket was carried into the middle of the farmyard, and a large full ale bowl was set upon it. All had ale to drink, this was in memory of the departed, and it was called a "farewell skål."

Family and friends processed across the fields to the graveyard for the burial. They then went back to the family home, where they had food, ale, and even dancing, probably similar to a "wake" in other cultures.

Flask, Valdres, Norway, 1781.
Vesterheim Norwegian-American Museum

Ale goose, Norway, 1830-1870.
Vesterheim Norwegian-American Museum

Silver beaker, Norway , 1841
Vesterheim Norwegian-American Museum

Silver beaker, Norway, 1816.
Vesterheim Norwegian-American Museum.
Luther College Collection

These examples show that ale drinking was connected with certain events and roles. Ale drinking made it easier to carry out those roles, but on the other hand, too much drinking could be a hindrance, so there was a need for moderation. The Haugean revival had a moderating influence on these celebrations as time went on, taking a strong stand against the use or excesses of alcohol. Women were generally more moderate in their imbibing of ale, and could help to keep the party in order.

Also there was a kind of internal control. Festive occasions were a part of country traditions, and the host did not want the events ruined by excessive drinking. The celebrations were very local, and everyone knew they would have to face their friends in days to come, and they did not want to be too embarrassed. And even the fiddler could help to moderate the occasion: if he played slow music, the people drank more; if he played fast, jolly music, people would dance more and drink less!

These customs persisted in the Norwegian countryside well up into the 19th century. People periodically brewed large amounts of ale, and drank quite freely at special events. However, the ale was said not to have had good keeping qualities, so they brewed and passed the ale bowl, and in general waited until the next big event for more ale. Some farmers grew a special patch of hops, which could be included in the brew, and this helped to preserve the ale.

Hard liquor (*brennevin*), most often aquavit (*akevitt*), was distilled from grain or potato, and flavored with caraway or other herbs or spices. Aquavit was available at some times, but was not the communal drink of festive occasions as was the place of ale. Because of shortage of grain, distilling in the countryside was prohibited from 1756 to 1816, and then again after 1845 because of so much public drunkenness. Aquavit did indeed have good shelf life, so drinking became more commonplace, less in quantity, but occurring throughout the year. Brandy was also sometimes purchased and was served in small silver cups, *tømlinger*, and was often warmed over the flame of a candle.

The very fact that thousands of ale bowls have survived, with interiors as well as exteriors still brightly painted, supports the theory that ale drinking was not a constant or everyday pattern. Norway was cold and life was hard in olden times. The celebrations and drinking of ale gave warmth and comfort and solidarity to the community through the years.

Silver cup (tomling), Norway, 1865.
Vesterheim Norwegian-American Museum

Ale bowl with rosemaling, Telemark, Norway, 1807 or 1867. Translated inscription: I used to stand in a green meadow and now I am a beautiful bowl.
Vesterheim Norwegian-American Museum

Spouted ale bowl, Norway, 1750-1800.
Vesterheim Norwegian-American Museum, Luther College Collection

Some journeys change you forever

By Lise Lian, textwriter,
Wittusen & Jensen AS, Oslo

Aquavit – A Historic Tradition

In April 1531, the Archbishop of Trondheim received a letter from Bergen, signed by the Danish Officer of the Crown, Eske Bille: "I send Your Grace some water called *Aqua vitae*. This water cures all types of internal diseases from which a human being may suffer."

The Norwegian Vikings who lived more than 500 years earlier were not, of course, strangers to alcohol. They drank mainly mead, but were known to have brought wine home from some of their numerous crusades abroad. The honour of having introduced *aqua vitae* to Norway must, however, be attributed to Archbishop Olav Engelbrektson of Trondheim.

The benefits of herbal remedies based on distilled spirits had long been recognized in Europe, where the Black Plague resulted in increasing demand for this particular "medicine." For many years, *aqua vitae* was used purely for medicinal purposes in Norway. It was distilled from grain and flavoured using a variety of herbs.

As the process of distillation became more widespread, distilling pans became an increasingly common sight in farmers' kitchens throughout the country. By now, it had become customary to take this "medicine" in Norway and its life-giving qualities were greatly appreciated by the scattered, hard-working inhabitants of this cold, barren country. A glass of aquavit was to be recommended prior to starting work in the fields or forests on cold, dark winter mornings. It is also worth mentioning that alcohol was the only drink which did not freeze in the cold Norwegian winter.

Linie aquavit.
Courtesy of Arcus AS

Gilde aquavit.
Courtesy of Arcus AS

*Olaus Magnus, Historia de gentibus
septentrionalibus, 1555.*

Løiten aquavit.
Courtesy of Arcus AS

As time went by, the many excellent reasons for enjoying aquavit gave rise to a somewhat exaggerated use of the spirit. This caused general concern and several legal restrictions were introduced, culminating in total prohibition, more than 200 years after the Archbishop had introduced the life-giving water. However, rather than being the result of Norwegian morality, it is far more likely that prohibition was brought about by lack of grain, not to mention the prospect of increased tax revenues. As a result of political pressure, prohibition was eventually lifted for a period, the aim allegedly being to improve the farmers' economy. The potato had now also appeared on the scene.

Museum of Danish America

The Grapes of the North

Wealthy Norwegians were known to have planted an exotic South American vegetable in their garden. It was known as Solanum Tuberosum – the potato. The vegetable was well suited to the Norwegian climate and soil. So well suited, in fact, that priests all over Norway praised its many virtues. The clergy considered themselves responsible for improving the farmers' living conditions. To quote a clergyman of former days,"The potato can be used in bread and as animal fodder, but is most suitable as raw material in the production of aquavit." High grain prices and the fact that potatoes yielded threefold, encouraged farmers to increase cultivation.

Some of the first written evidence of the potato being used as a raw material in alcohol production dates from 1791, when a certain Halvor Rasmussen Wang from Trondheim sent a petition to the King of Denmark, asking permission to produce alcohol from potatoes. He argued that his intention, apart from establishing his own business, was to help Norwegian farmers make better use of their agricultural produce.

Improving the quality of both stills and alcohol became another important issue and it has since been discovered that the famous aquavit producer Jørgen B. Lysholm corresponded with experts in Germany. There, Joh. Heinr. Lebrecht Pistorius researched new techniques and subsequently published a paper describing a new device for the distilling of cleaner and stronger alcohol in 1832.

Although the first distilleries had been established by 1800, it was only with the improvement of distillation techniques, combined with the introduction of the potato, that the spirit industry really flourished. Alcohol produced from potatoes is clean, neutral and well-rounded, highly suitable for extracting aromas from the Nordic flora.

The spices used for creating the aquavit before it is shipped.
Courtesy of Arcus AS

A Genuine Norwegian Taste

Alcohol is quite unique as regards extracting flavour and aroma from herbs. The discovery of this fact lead to significant progress within the field of medicine and an abundance of recipes. The number of ingredients employed could often exceed 100, and this gave rise to such expressions as "The greater the number of herbs and spices, the greater the number of diseases cured" or "The worse the taste, the better the results."

From being used purely for medicinal purposes, alcohol soon became more widespread, drunk to ease the strains of a heavy working day. Herbs and spices thereby assumed a new role – that of disguising the taste of simple, home-made alcohol and improving this life-giving elixir. To understand why this was of such great importance, one need look no further than to the highly unsatisfactory quality of the farmers' primitive kitchen stills. It was also quite natural for Norwegians of the time to pick caraway, juniper, angelica, pimpinella (anise) and hypericum in the fields and forests.

The year 1776 marked the publication of the first document to examine the making of aquavit and fruit wines in detail. The author, Christopher Hammer, was an educated landowner and senior official dedicated to "chymia applicata," to use his own expression. His name will always be closely linked with Norwegian aquavit. Caraway aquavit and cinnamon aquavit, as the names imply, only contained one herb, while other aquavits could contain a mixture of herbs, roots, seeds or fruits of aniseed, angelica, wormwood, juniper, calamus, lemon balm, curled mint etc.

Caraway is still the most important herb in aquavit production, but dill, aniseed, sweet fennel, coriander and other related plants also play an important role. The long, light days and short, cool nights which are characteristic of the Norwegian summer, produce caraway of an exceptionally high quality. This may well explain the plant's dominant role in aquavit production. Today, a number of farmers grow caraway to be used in aquavit in the fresh, unpolluted Norwegian countryside.

The sherry casks used for maturing Linie aquavit on land and at sea.

Courtesy of Arcus AS

Unique Maturation in Casks

Norwegian aquavit differs from the other Nordic aquavits because it is matured in sherry casks. The process is more or less identical to that used in the production of whisky and cognac and places Norwegian aquavit in a class of its own.

Maturation is an important and costly part of aquavit production. It starts with the importing of 500-litre sherry casks from Jerez in Spain. The casks have been used in the production of Oloroso sherry for five to ten years. They give the aquavit its golden colour, the remains of the sherry give it a pleasant sweetness and the white American or Spanish oak provides hints of wood and vanilla.

During this period of maturation, considerable changes occur in the composition and character of the aquavit. A certain amount of oxidation alters the aroma of the herbs and spices. The alcohol extracts substances from the oak which also contribute to the chemical processes. The rawer, more volatile and somewhat aggressive aspects of the spirit vanish however, as some of the alcohol evaporates. We say that this is how the angels get their share and we have every reason to believe that they are very happy angels.

The maturation process follows a progression which varies for each brand. The clue is finding the perfect time to end the process of maturation, characteristic to each special aquavit brand. The best known of all Norwegian aquavits is Lysholm Linie Aquavit, famous both for its unique maturation process and for its refined taste. It is made according to the traditional recipe of its creator, Jørgen B. Lysholm, and is matured while sailing around the world, crossing the Equator (the "line" or *linie*) twice.

Jørgen Lysholm, the father of
Linie aquavit.
Courtesy of Arcus AS

Jørgen B. Lysholm
(1796–1843)

Jørgen B. Lysholm

The name Jørgen Bernhoft Lysholm has become synonymous with Norwegian aquavit. However, the story really started with Jørgen's aunt, Catharina Lysholm, who built the brig *Trondhiems Prøve* in 1780, in collaboration with her brother, an important tradesman. There is proof that this sailing ship visited the East Indies in 1805 with a new product, potato spirit, as well as various other types of merchandise on board. This was a purely speculative enterprise, undertaken in the hope of opening new markets. When this attempt at selling potato spirit failed, the cargo was returned to Norway. Throughout the whole voyage, the potato spirit was transported as deck cargo. On arrival in Norway in 1807, it was discovered that the voyage had vastly improved the taste of the aquavit. This fact was kept a closely-guarded secret by the Lysholm family for many years.

Jørgen B. Lysholm himself was still a young man when he inherited his father's soap factory near Trondheim and rebuilt it as a distillery in 1821. He had recently completed studies in chemistry and technology in Berlin. A short while later, he moved the distillery to the centre of Trondheim, built a new factory and offices and enlarged the warehouses. When Jørgen B. died, his son Nicolai took over and, at a later date, his younger son Claus Krabbe continued what was by now an important business, producing nationally and internationally renowned aquavit.

Responsibility for the production of Lysholm Linie Aquavit was taken over by the state monopoly on its establishment in 1922, but the secret Lysholm recipe and its traditional production methods were never altered. Even today, we are proud to continue the tradition of producing Norway's oldest and most prestigious aquavit brand exactly as it has been produced for more than 200 years. Today, the Linie Aquavit label still carries the signature of its creator.

Trondhjems Prøve, the original ship that sailed back and forth to Australia and gave the sailors a chance to discover Linie aquavit.

Courtesy of Arcus AS

Some Journeys Change You Forever

Over the years, there have been many theories as to how Jørgen B. Lysholm happened to discover the process of maturation which makes his Linie Aquavit so special. We do know that thanks to his aunt's efforts, the idea of exporting aquavit already existed. The logbook from her ship, *Trondhiems Prøve*, states that it passed the equator on 24th October 1805, bound for the East Indies. Five casks of aquavit were later returned in 1807, unsold.

The positive effect of such a sea voyage on the maturation of the alcohol was commercialised by the Lysholm family, owners of Nordstjernen and Gymer of Trondhjem. Gymer sailed around the world via Australia and her skipper was a marine officer by the name of David Lysholm, 3rd generation of the famous family.

The Lysholm Aquavit's unique maturation process remained a carefully guarded secret for generations. Today, scientific knowledge confirms the value of the old tradition: the length of the trip, constant gentle rolling, varying temperatures and sea air on deck combine to perform a sophisticated kind of sorcery, smoothing and enhancing the flavour of the alcohol.

Sailing ships have long since vanished, but Linie Aquavit still crosses the equator. Since 1927, the Norwegian ship-owner Wilh. Wilhelmsen has assumed responsibility for this precious process. ISO 9000 specifications stipulate that the barrels must be transported as deck cargo. Each month new loads of oak barrels embark upon a four and a half month journey, taking them to 35 countries and crossing the Equator twice during the voyage. At any given time, more than a thousand Linie Aquavit casks are maturing as deck cargo on the oceans. Every bottle of Linie Aquavit carries details of its voyage around the world via Australia on the reverse of its label. Even more importantly, every mouthful of Linie Aquavit contains memories of its sea voyage.

Old-style Linie bottle.
Courtesy of Arcus AS

Making the Most of Linie Aquavit

Aquavit is Norway's national drink. Not only because of its long history, but also because aquavit belongs on the Norwegian table, a fact recognised by traditionalists, modernists and connoisseurs alike. For confirmation of this fact, one need look no further than to the rapid increase in sales, surpassing that of any other type of alcohol.

The different flavours of Norwegian aquavits provide a fitting accompaniment to Norway's traditional dishes, including salted, smoked or cured meats, pickled, fermented or dried food, smoked salmon, sea-food and other specialities. It is particularly beneficial as an accompaniment to pork and other rich, fatty dishes.

Fatty and salty foods warrant the use of a digestif. Traditionally, aquavit is drunk as a chaser with beer, as a kind of "schnapps." The aquavit should be drunk after the beer and not before, so that its delicate taste lingers in the mouth. The oils and herbs present in aquavit have the same effects on digestion as they had in the olden days when it was drunk purely for medicinal purposes.

Norwegians believe that the subtle flavour of Linie Aquavit is best appreciated when the product is served at room temperature or, if necessary, slightly chilled. Irrespective of local culinary traditions, tastes and habits – for centuries the aquavit's capacity for aiding digestion has been appreciated in countries all over the world. It can either be used as an apèritif before the meal, as a digestif following the meal, or quite simply between courses. Or why not try one of our recipes? *(See pages 66)*

Julmiddag (Christmas lunch) hosted at the
Café Idrott, 1913.
Swedish American Museum

CHAPTER 5

Swedish Chicago: Temperance Cafes and Speakeasies

By Veronica L. S. Robinson, Curator,
Swedish American Museum

In the 19th and early 20th centuries, temperance movements were building momentum in both the United States and Sweden. These movements, mostly rooted in religious pietistism, sought to prohibit the consumption of intoxicating liquors, or at least moderate their use, for the betterment of society. In the mid-1800s, the cause of Swedish temperance was mainly directed and supported by the upper classes of society. The Swedish Temperance Society could boast of supporters like the famous singer, Jenny Lind as well as military and religious leaders. This first movement was aimed mainly at moderating the use of alcohol, rather than complete abstention, and while it gained some ground during the 1840s and 1850s, it lost broader interest after 1855, when the Licensing Act outlawed home distilling, cutting per-capita consumption. In the 1860s, the largest Swedish temperance group, the Swedish Temperance Society, began to devote most of its activities to educational literature rather than political agitation.

Bottle, SAL Aquavit, 1928. Label inscription:
"Genuine S.A.L. Aquavit produced in Sweden by
Aktiebolaget-Vin-Spritcentralen Stockholm.
Specially flavored and bottled for the Swedish
American Line-4/5 Quart 80 Proof."

Swedish American Museum

In 1879, Olof Bergström, who had emigrated from Sweden to the U.S., retuned to Gothenburg bringing with him ideas from the American temperance movement and founded the first Swedish chapter of the Independent Order of Good Templars, a temperance organization with roots in New York. This new organization differed from earlier temperance movements in Sweden as it found support among the working classes and promoted total abstinence rather than moderation of alcohol. By the 1880s, several more temperance organizations had started work in Sweden, including the Order of Templars, the Swedish Blue Ribbon Society, the Temperance Order of Verdandi and the White Ribbon Society, an off-shoot of the popular American group, Women's Christian Temperance Union. Membership in and support for these groups reached its peak around 1910. These groups focused mainly on education and healthful alternative activities to drinking such as sports and games. A slogan created by the Swedish Temperance Society advocated "Away with the drink habit, forward with the reading habit."

The rise in popularity of these temperance groups significantly overlapped with a period of mass emigration from Sweden, when over 1 million people left the country, usually bound for the United States. While this connection with the U.S. helped usher in the new temperance movement in Sweden, many of these new temperance supporters shortly left for the United States, strengthening the movement in America. Some of the first Swedish clubs founded by immigrants in Chicago were centered on the cause of temperance. Additionally, Swedes founded numerous Independent Order of Good Templars lodges, (later renamed, International Order of Good Templars,) in the Chicago-area.

Not every Swede, however, supported the cause of temperance. Many Swedes and Swedish immigrants to the U.S. supported the manufacture and consumption of alcohol. Aquavit, *brännvin*, *glögg*, beer and other alcoholic drinks were part of traditional holidays and celebrations and remained so for many among the Swedish population. Many secular Swedish clubs in Chicago included bars in their clubhouses and served alcohol at events and celebrations. Chicago was also home to many Swedish-owned taverns – including Gengler's Tavern in the Swedish enclave of Andersonville, and Lundqvist Tavern in Lakeview, both on Chicago's north side.

When the 18th Amendment to the United States Constitution went into effect in 1920, prohibiting the sale, manufacture, and transportation of intoxicating liquors, the Swedes in the U.S. were divided on the issue. Swedish-American opinion on the temperance movement as well as the Prohibition amendment can be illustrated by two very different organizations; Café Idrott, a cooperative Swedish Temperance Café, and Simon's Tavern, which was a speakeasy – an illegal drinking spot – during the prohibition era.

(above and left) Carl Lundquist's tavern, Chicago.
Swedish American Museum

Café Idrott, Chicago, 1930.
Swedish American Museum

Café Idrott

Café Idrott was a cooperative social club and café in Chicago's north side neighborhood of Lakeview, one of the heavily Swedish neighborhoods in the city in the early 20th century. A group of young Swedish Chicagoans met in 1913 to organize the temperance club on the third floor of a building at 930 Belmont Avenue. The group decided to name the club "Idrott," likely after the social movement in Sweden toward increased athletic programming, but may also have been named for a presumed ancient Viking sport. The full name of the organization was *Kooperativa Nykterhetskafeet Idrott* or the Cooperative Temperance Café "Idrott" in English.

Interior dining area of Café Idrott, 1913.
Swedish American Museum

Photo of manager and wait staff at
Café Idrott, 1912.
Swedish American Museum

The café seems to have been inspired by the later temperance movement in Sweden in which supporters of temperance sought to supplant the activity of drinking with other more wholesome activities such as sports, games and educational pursuits. The founders of the café intended the organization to function for the purposes of the preservation of Swedish identity, abstention from intoxicating liquors, as well as intellectual and physical pursuits. The cooperative maintained the restaurant and café and a bakery as well as a library containing Swedish books magazines and current Swedish-language newspapers from Sweden and the United States. The café hosted lectures and debates in the Swedish language and offered meeting rooms to other area clubs, such as the Verdandi Educational League and the Lakeview Swedish Cultural Society. As late as 1930, the annual report for the café, which outlined financials and programming, was printed in the Swedish language.

The café operated on the Rochdale cooperative principals which allowed it to accrue only minimal profit on the goods they sold and any profit was reinvested into the café for improvements, educational programs, and the growth of the library. Additionally, those profits could be donated to benefit other like-minded organizations, or to organize educational programming, or exhibits on Swedish art and culture.

There is little existing evidence that Café Idrott consistently campaigned for the cause of temperance or prohibition, but seems to have served more as an alternative club and meeting house for Swedes who abstained from liquor. Alcohol was neither served nor allowed within the cafe. A menu from around 1931 prominently displays the warning "Intoxicating liquors strictly prohibited" near the bottom of the page. According to one newspaper article, in 1931, Café Idrott did host a debate between two attorneys on issues of prohibition.

The café was successful enough that it was able to open a second location in another heavily Swedish neighborhood on Chicago's north side, Andersonville. According to a 1925 issue of Svenska Kurien, the new Café Idrott opened in 1925 at 5248 N. Clark Street. Interestingly, in 1976, this building became the first home for the Swedish American Museum in Chicago.

Café Idrott appears to have had continued success into the 1930s. Swedish language newspaper articles mention art exhibits in the 1930s and growth of the café appears evident in the 1930 annual report. According to an article by Henry Bengston in a 1962 edition of the Swedish Pioneer Historical Quarterly, "the 1930 Depression years swept away Café Idrott, as they did most of the businesses on Belmont and elsewhere." The last mention of Café Idrott that the author could find was in a 1938 edition of the Chicago Tribune. The café building in Lakeview was demolished in 2006 to make way for an expanded CTA Rapid Transit station.

Simon's tavern, Chicago, present day.
Swedish American Museum

Simon's Tavern

Today, Simon's Tavern is a friendly, local watering hole located in Chicago's Andersonville neighborhood, one of the most well-known historically Swedish enclaves in the city. The tavern sits across the street from the Swedish American Museum on Clark Street and welcomes visitors with a neon sign of a fish wearing a "Viking" helmet while holding a martini. The sign is a play on words; the fish represents a "pickled herring" – a famous Swedish delicacy. The sign advertises that the Tavern was established in 1934, but the history of this bar goes back further than that – when it was a 'speakeasy' during Prohibition.

Simon's Tavern, Chicago, present day.
Swedish American Museum

No Name Club, Simon's Tavern Basement.
Swedish American Museum

The colorful history of Simon's Tavern begins with Simon Lundberg, a Swedish immigrant to the United States who left the province of Småland in the early 20th century. Lundberg became a full citizen by fighting for the United States during the First World War. After his service in the armed forces, he traveled out west to Colorado to work for the railroads, but always dreamed of owning his own business. In 1922, he heard of many Swedes moving to the Andersonville neighborhood on Chicago's north side. He moved into the area that year and opened up a café reputedly called the Berwyn Food Shop. The legend according to Scott Martin, the bar's current owner, goes like this:

"A couple of gentlemen sat at his counter one day and ordered coffee. And as the coffee was placed in front of them, one gentleman opened up his overcoat and took something out which he unscrewed the top of and poured it into the coffee, and he slid the coffee cup to Simon, suggesting he taste it. So, Simon tasted it and he said 'oh, that's a pretty good whiskey!' And they said, 'Well we can get you a regular supply, put the word on the street and nobody will bother you.' And Simon said 'ok.'"

By 1926, Simon's "coffee" had become so popular that he was able to purchase another building at 5210 N. Clark (the bar's present location,) and open a second location of his café. He moved his family to the apartment on the second floor of that building in the same year. In 1929, at the urging of some of his dedicated customers – who wanted the whiskey without the coffee – he set up a club in the basement of the building with five wooden tables, a line of whiskey bottles along the wall, and a door to the back alley with a peep-hole and the name "N. N. Club." Scott admits "Comically, it stands for the No Norwegians Club, but literally, it did stand for the No Name Club." Here, many Swedish-American men sat, drank whiskey and talked about politics, business and women, according to Roy Lundberg, Simon's only child.

1933 brought about the repeal of Prohibition with the 21st Amendment to the United States Constitution. Lundberg worked quickly, remodeling the first floor of his building into the tavern it is today. He modeled the interior after the famous French steamship the S.S. Normandie, then one of the most luxurious ocean liners of the time. Current owner, Scott Martin purchased the bar from Lundburg's son, Roy, in 1994. Martin had grown up in the Andersonville neighborhood and was very fond of the bar; his father, Tom, had taken him to Simon's for his twenty-first birthday as well as on other celebratory occasions.

Martin has many remnants of the original speakeasy – three wooden tables, the old N. N. Club door, decorative paint on the basement walls and countless stories. Martin continues to maintain the Swedish character of the bar – serving aquavit, Jepson's Malört and house-made glögg – served warm, as dictated by tradition, but also in an iced "slushie" form during the annual Andersonville Midsommarfest in June. Simon's Tavern also serves and array of craft beers on tap and in bottles and serves as a popular spot for neighborhood friends as well as new visitors to the city.

Swedes and Swedish Americans, like many other nationalities, were incredibly divided on the issue of intoxicating liquors; in Chicago, there was always room for each opinion as well as gathering spot for each. Whether you wanted intellectual pursuits without the interference of alcohol or a good conversation over whiskey, early 20th century Chicago had a club for you.

Old Ballard Liquor Co., Seattle, Washington.
Photo by Jason Brooks

Blue-Collar Ballard: Aquavit with a Budweiser Chaser

An interview with Lexi, *founder/proprietor of Old Ballard Liquor Co.,*
by Kirsten Olsen, *Exhibitions Coordinator at the Nordic Heritage Museum*

In Seattle's traditionally Scandinavian neighborhood of Ballard, the heart of "Old Ballard" is Ballard Avenue. Now a designated Historic District, Ballard Avenue was home to many of the neighborhood's drinking establishments from its very beginning. Located just a few blocks away from the docks, fishing fleets, lumber and shingle mills, the neighborhood was the domain of fishermen, crabbers, dock workers, welders, pipefitters, and other tradesmen. The bars and saloons that were the gathering place for these men were a rough and rowdy environment. Drinking and gambling became such a problem that in 1904, in an attempt to prevent the activities for 24 hours, the mayor officially closed the city of Ballard for a day.

Old Ballard Liquor Co., Seattle, Washington.
Photo by Jason Brooks

When Lexi, the founder and proprietor of the Old Ballard Liquor Company, was looking for a neighborhood to establish her new micro-distillery, she chose this neighborhood precisely for its blue-collar and Scandinavian roots. She honors the neighborhood's heritage in many ways, including offering a 10% discount for maritime workers and Scandinavian-language speakers.

We stopped by the Old Ballard Liquor Company on a busy afternoon before Christmas to ask Lexi some questions about her distillery and aquavit:

Why aquavit?

Lexi: I turned 18 while living in Sweden (the drinking age) and fell in love with aquavit. We've always had a lot of aquavit in this area of the U.S., and as imported Scandinavian aquavits started disappearing off the shelves over the past eight years or so, the missing imports were taking their toll on Americans' ability to experience and understand aquavit.

When I decided in 2011 to start a distillery, one of my primary goals was to reintroduce Americans to the incredible range of flavors found in Aquavits across Scandinavia. Aquavit has a much broader flavor palette than any other type of liquor, and as the diversity of aquavit styles disappeared from the U.S. market, I saw a real need to address this widening gap in our liquor choices.

By offering a diverse range of aquavits that are representative of the wide variety of styles you'd find in Scandinavia, I've been able to provide products that the local Scandinavian population enjoys and supports while introducing Americans to a wonderful spirit that they wouldn't otherwise be able to experience.

What qualities of aquavit attracted you to making it a core part of your production?

Lexi: I have a great love of history and culture. As I see the Scandinavian culture disappearing here in Ballard, it makes me deeply sad; this is how in my own small way, I can keep it alive, service a fading community, and maybe make that culture cool enough that young people will become interested.

Aquavit isn't well represented in the American distilling market. Although that's slowly starting to change, at the time of this interview, there are only two distilleries in the U.S. making aquavit as their primary product line. Most domestic aquavit is made by distilleries that have their core line in more conventional products (whiskey, gin, vodka) and make an aquavit as a one-off.

It's risky to put all of your investment into an unconventional product like this, but I think that we're both making it because we love it and want to share it, not because it's just a commodity.

How would you describe the history of aquavit in the Ballard community?

Lexi: Ballard is an old Scandinavian fishing community. It's one of three deeply Scandinavian enclaves in Washington State. Poulsbo is a small Norwegian port village over on the peninsula, and the third is Stanwood, a farming community about an hour north of Seattle. My mother and

Tavern interior, Ballard neighborhood of Seattle, early 20th century.
Nordic Heritage Museum

Old Ballard Liquor Co., Seattle, Washington.
Photo by Jason Brooks

grandmother both grew up in Stanwood and my family goes back five generations in the Skagit Valley. I don't have particularly strong Scandinavian blood, but I consider myself culturally Scandinavian because we've been part of that community for so long. Aquavit was consumed extensively within those communities, but not necessarily so much outside of them. A popular saying would have been, "it's that drink the square-heads like."

Down here in Ballard specifically, all the way up through the 1980s, we had a really rough and tumble industrial fishing community. There were pipe-fitters and welders, fishermen, captains; guys that had seen a lot. These are very, very dangerous jobs, even when you're working on the docks – so these were tough guys. There was a time in Ballard when it was all Scandinavians, the families living higher up on the hill with tidy yards and Norwegian flags, and the blue collar guys were downtown. In those days you couldn't walk down Ballard Avenue after 10:00 without getting into a fight; everybody was drunk by then and out trying to pick fights. These guys would get off their jobs at 4:00 or 5:00 in the evening and head down to the old dive bars on Ballard Ave and order a shot of aquavit – their shot instead of whiskey was aquavit – and a beer. But the beer was always the cheapest beer that they had at the bar, which was usually a Budweiser in a can. So I actually have a "cocktail" that is called the Ballard Standard. It's s a shot of aquavit served alongside a Budweiser in a can.

The neighborhood of Ballard started gentrifying about five or six years ago. It was re-zoned from light-industrial to mixed-use residential and commercial, and, being fairly close to downtown, over the period of 18 to 24 months, it suddenly just flipped, it was if somebody put the whole neighborhood on a pivot, turned it upside down, and a new neighborhood sprung up in its place. It was a huge shift; a lot of that shift happened because all the Scandinavians are now old Scandinavians. There's no young blood; there are no young Swedes or young Norwegians in the community anymore; it's people's grandparents. So as time goes on and properties change hands, bringing in a new population, what we're seeing is this whole new community coming into Ballard that doesn't have much experience with Scandinavian culture.

Is aquavit still culturally significant?

Lexi: Yes, but I fear that it's getting less so. What I see is that as the Scandinavian population in Ballard is dying off, less ex-patriate Scandinavians are coming to purchase aquavit and more and more of their kids are. It's becoming something that's consumed only at Christmas because it's a tradition, not so much because it's something that they drink for itself.

Scandinavian communities tend to place a high value on tradition and can be a bit insular sometimes. I haven't found much encouragement for newcomers to try aquavit, so it's disappearing here simply for lack of sales and interest. In order to keep it on the country's larger cultural radar, it's important to court bartenders and the general public with products that they can get excited about.

When, where, with whom, is aquavit consumed?

Lexi: Around here: usually at Christmas, by Scandinavian families. I'm working hard to change that by pursuing a very aggressive cocktail program with local bars and bartenders.

An important distinction to make with aquavit is that in Scandinavia, it's always and only taken neat, but Americans nearly always drink it in cocktails. Typically, a Scandinavian aquavit will be higher in proof but lighter in flavor than its American counterparts. Domestic U.S. aquavits tend to be richer in flavor because they have to stand up in a cocktail, where the subtler imported versions would disappear. Native Scandinavians can be horrified that we cocktail with aquavit. I've had some very funny conversations with some appalled Swedes about my cocktail program.

Because of that, the way that it's consumed really varies depending on your community. Scandinavian families will drink it neat with Christmas dinner, while local bartenders will put it into their craft cocktail rotations for Saturday nights. It's very situationally-dependent.

What role do you hope to play in continuing, expanding, or evolving the use of aquavit?

Lexi: I would really like to see Americans learn about aquavit. I believe that once people understand the diversity and range of flavors aquavit incorporates, and the basics of different regional styles, they will start to enjoy and appreciate it. I'm all about education and making sure that customers have enough information to make an informed decision. Finding opportunities to get educational information out there – like through this exhibition – are incredibly valuable.

Getting average American bartenders on board is really important. Bartenders are kind of the front-line of consumer educational opportunity and the more professionals who understand and enjoy aquavit, the more exposure it will get in the U.S., and by extension, more varieties will be available to choose from. It can't just be high end craft bartenders though – aquavit is a product that should be enjoyed everywhere, at every level. Any bar in the U.S. that has a bottle of gin on the shelf should also have at least one bottle of aquavit.

Because there's so little information out there for people to learn from, I've worked to put together a comprehensive aquavit educational workshop that is

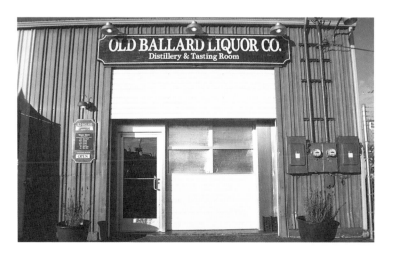

Old Ballard Liquor Co., Seattle, Washington.
Photo by Jill Rachel Evans

offered to professionals and private groups on a regular basis. We discuss the different styles and flavors of aquavit throughout Scandinavia and regional differences in the U.S., then taste through a number of examples of both imported and domestic aquavits. Giving people an opportunity to actually try the variety and discuss the differences has really been effective, and I hope to continue spreading the word.

What has been the response to your aquavit production?

Lexi: It's been incredibly well received. The Scandinavian population in Seattle has been very supportive. The general population needs a lot more education and exposure, which equates to slower growth outside of the immediate ex-patriate community.

The response from native Scandinavians versus first or second generation Scandinavian-Americans has been very different. For the most part the response has been overwhelmingly positive from the Scandinavian community. I've worked very hard to involve members of that community in every step of the production and tasting process. We go through about 40 tests before we settle on a recipe for a particular product, and the last stage is a lunch and tasting panel where we taste the top 10 to 15 recipes along with food and without food, so we have a food pairing and a non-food pairing. We include Scandinavian ex-pats, bartenders, a good mix of the whole customer base, in those tasting panels, definitely making sure that those communities understand that they're involved and we're not ignoring their input.

Sometimes folks from Scandinavia can be staunch brand loyalists, and when they try a domestic aquavit, occasionally you do get someone who says something like "Well, I only drink O.P. Anderson." That's fine – everyone likes what they like – but it's important to note that if aquavit in general becomes popular in the U.S., then imports like O.P Anderson are likely to become available again. A rising tide lifts all boats, as they say.

Who is the audience?

Lexi: It depends. As mentioned before, U.S. and Scandinavian aquavits have some core differences because of how they're taken, and so on to who drinks them.

I try to hit a balance between authentic flavors but made for American bartenders. Instead of reinventing the product, I take those familiar sets of aquavit styles and flavors, twist them a bit to make them local to this area (like using Alder wood to age my Norwegian-style aquavits instead of oak or sherry casks), and then making them strong enough to be used in a cocktail – but not changing them to the point of unrecognizability. It's a tough balance.

Sometimes consumers who are accustomed to typical Scandinavian brands don't like how strong the domestics taste, but for the most part, they understand and recognize the authenticity – and usually appreciate the thoughtfulness that goes into each flavor. The fact that Gamle Ode and Old Ballard Liquor Co. are both doing a variety of styles and flavors to meet different preferences helps, as well as being able to draw direct parallels to recognized brands in Scandinavia.

Old Ballard Liquor Co., Seattle, Washington.
Photo by Jason Brooks

U.S. bartenders and liquor geeks are just starting to get into this product, but without a large marketing budget or distribution, it's tough to get new, small batch liquor into the hands of enough people to really make a dent. Old Ballard does have a small, loyal following who come in every month or so to see what's new, which is pretty great.

There is also a lot of aquavit on the shelves here in Seattle, since four of the 10 U.S. distillers making aquavit are in this area , so the Seattle audience is there already; it's more a matter of getting people to change their perceptions of what aquavit can be.

There's also this weird thing with perceived value regarding aquavit. It's not something that Americans have had much exposure to, yet hip bartenders often have these really vehement ideas about what defines 'good' or 'bad' aquavit when they don't really know anything about it. I haven't figured out how to approach that yet.

Is it people who were already aware of aquavit and sought a local source?

Lexi: Loads of people here already know about aquavit, but most have only tried a couple of local licorice-forward ones without realizing there are other choices. The Scandinavians that I've dealt with so far have been people who are unhappy with the existing aquavit selection available in town and have been looking for something more familiar – especially those communities not represented by a domestic aquavit style already, like the Danes, who don't have anything available on the U.S. market right now that's comparable to Aalborg Taffel.

I think most of the Seattle-area Scandinavians are aware that there are locally produced aquavits, and typically will find Old Ballard products through word of mouth. I wouldn't say that Scandinavians are actively looking for a 'local source'- because of a tendency toward brand loyalty to the products back home. But like the growth of any craft industry, that's all about encouraging people to try something local and handmade instead of corporate. You see that happening in Sweden and Norway too, with their own new craft aquavit distilleries competing against the big national brands for customers.

Are you making "aquavit converts"?

Lexi: Absolutely! In the tasting room especially, where we can chat and educate and taste. People will come in for a different product – like vodka or liqueur – and walk out with aquavit and a handful of recipes and ideas. Bartenders especially get behind the history and complexity of this spirit once they're exposed to it. It comes down again to education – if someone hands you a bottle without a story, it's just a bottle that you might not ever even open. But the story and the history provide a context that makes it exciting and fun. Getting bartenders and stores to really understand aquavit so that they can in turn educate customers is going to be the key to aquavit's continued success and availability in the United States.

Denmark is a Nation of Individualists

By Claus Toftkjær, Category Manager,
Arcus AS, Copenhagen

Even though the country covers less than 30,000 square miles, there are great differences among the Danes. Although it is only 229 miles from north to south, there can be a long way between each of them. And even though they speak the same language, they sometimes have trouble understanding each other.

But there is something that is able to erase these differences, shorten the distances and even make speech superfluous, thus eliminating any misunderstanding.

To find it, one must home in on the distillate of the Danish DNA – the space where fashion, zeitgeist, superficiality, social class, generational difference and political persuasion have evaporated, and only the Danish essence remains.

…and the Danish essence can be bottled.

It consists mainly of wheat, water, herbs and knowledge – and this blend may sound very simple.

But it isn't.

Because in addition to wheat, water, knowledge and herbs, the essence contains an ingredient that not even the richest men, women or hedge funds can acquire.

It has soul.

Jubilæums (Jubilee) Aquavit.
Courtesy of Arcus AS

Foundation stone, 1929.
Courtesy of Arcus AS

The Aalborg Aquavit sign. Aalborg 1943.
Courtesy of Arcus AS

Collecting the dregs. Urbansgade. Aalborg. 1925.
Courtesy of Arcus AS

Soul created through generations of fiery passion for creating the finest product of its kind.

It is 170 years of history that is poured into small glasses when the Danes gather with friends and family from near and far to breathe new life in to old traditions.

It is this soul that is used to add depth to encounters with new acquaintances.

It is this soul that they gather around on special occasions already in the calendar – or moments they define as something special themselves.

Even before it hits your taste buds and its sharp coolness turns into a blessed inner warmth, it has already broken down all barriers between young and old, fortunate and less-fortunate.

It is this soul, which at once creates intense presence around the moment – and reminds us all, of what once was – and what is yet to come.

It is this soul that unites us.

And that makes words superfluous.

Mine, as well.

Skål by Aalborg Akvavit!

Turnblad Mansion.
American Swedish Institute

Sharing Cocktails and Culture at The American Swedish Institute

By Krista Ulman, Interpretive Planner,
American Swedish Institute

In 1929, Swedish-American immigrant and wealthy newspaper publisher Swan Turnblad donated his castle-like Minneapolis home to create The American Institute for Swedish Art, Literature, and Science. Over eight decades later, thousands of people visit each year for exhibits, public programs, and private events.

A teetotaler with a small family, Turnblad was never one to host large social gatherings, and there's no record of him ever serving alcohol to guests. He met his wife, Christina Nilsson, at a meeting of a Minneapolis temperance organization, and he seemingly held strong anti-alcohol views throughout his life.

Still, Turnblad recognized the significance of alcohol in both Swedish and American culture. The mansion he built originally included plans for a wine cellar, probably to increase the home's resale value. And the organization Turnblad founded, now the American Swedish Institute, has long served alcohol as one way of upholding Swedish traditions. Longstanding clubs and affiliated organizations such as *Punschklubben* have gathered in Turnblad's mansion for decades to share spirits and stories. And every summer for many years, ASI has held a crayfish dinner, where a host teaches hundreds of guests how to pull apart crayfish and properly *skål*. Partygoers giddy from aquavit lift their voices in raucous Swedish drinking songs, exuberantly connecting to their heritage.

With a campus expansion in 2012, ASI now features a restaurant that hosts a popular weekly happy hour. The museum's curator regularly takes visitors on cocktail tours through the mansion. And several times a year, thousands of revelers descend on the Institute for a night of dancing, music, art, and delightful food and drinks: Cocktails at the Castle.

Portrait of Swan J. Turnblad of Minneapolis, MN.
Oil painting by Christian von Schneidau.
circa 1930.
The American Swedish Institute

The annual Crayfish Party at the American
Swedish Institute in Minneapolis.
Photo courtesy of the American Swedish Institute

Staff sometimes wonder what Turnblad would think if he could see the American Swedish Institute today. What thoughts would run through his head as he watched thousands of people line up for Cocktails at the Castle? Would he glare at the revelers drinking beer on his lawn? Would he gasp at entertainers juggling flaming batons? Would he call the police to file a noise complaint?

Or would Swan Turnblad look at the staff serving cocktails and feel his heart bursting with pride? Perhaps he would admire their innovative approach to bringing people together. After all, he did the same thing himself.

Turnblad made his riches through the newspaper industry, in which he started as a young typesetter. Swedish language newspaper *Svenska Amerikanska Posten* launched in Minneapolis in 1885 as a four-page weekly devoted to prohibition and the temperance movement. Publisher Nils Peter Lind's tough stance on alcohol won the paper few subscribers. Turnblad was hired as manager less than two years after the newspaper debuted, charged with increasing subscription and advertising revenues.

Although Turnblad sympathized with Lind's anti-alcohol views, he deliberately chose to soften the newspaper's focus on temperance in order to broaden its general appeal. Turnblad also enlarged *Posten* to twenty pages, expanded the number of subscribers, and fixated on the paper's design, content, and production technology. By October 1897, he had become the owner of *Svenska Amerikanska Posten*, which he had shaped into the leading Swedish-language newspaper in the United States.

Posten became a key way for Swedish immigrants to connect with their homeland and maintain their Swedish identities. Ordinary people contributed stories and poetry, and shared news across the Atlantic. The more people subscribed, the more important Posten became as an anchor for the Swedish community.

Just as Posten brought the Swedish immigrant community together, the American Swedish Institute aims to be a gathering place for all people to share experiences around themes of culture, migration, the environment, and the arts, informed by enduring links to Sweden. Part of that mission involves introducing new audiences to ASI. While the Institute has long served alcohol at special events, innovative new programs such as Cocktails at the Castle utilize spirits and entertainment to share Swedish culture with millennials who might never have seen a *dala* horse before. Visitors come to Cocktails at the Castle because it's a great party, but along the way they explore Swedish art, learn the Swedish language, and acquire a greater understanding of historic and contemporary Swedish culture. Part of that culture is shared through drink, as partygoers sip aquavit cocktails and learn the proper way to *skål*. But the libations also serve as an entry point, an accessible way for people who know little about Sweden to start learning and engaging.

So if Swan Turnblad were alive today, he might grouse about high heels clicking on his wooden floors, but he would also recognize the importance of using parties, and even alcohol, as a way to expand people's access to Swedish culture. After all, he softened his own views on alcohol in order to expand his Swedish newspaper's audience. And this man who mostly kept to himself ultimately donated his home to become a museum and cultural center for all people. Who knows? Perhaps Turnblad would even attend one of ASI's parties, and we could all lift a glass and *skål!* to his incredible philanthropy.

Recipes

Viking Beer, Christmas Ale and Glögg

Viking Ale

Recipe from J.W. Kent

Ingredients for a 5-gallon batch:

11 lbs. Pale Malt (Maris Otter or Golden Promise)

2 lbs. Rye Malt

1 lb. Munich Malt

12 oz. Special B

3 oz. Peat smoked Malt

1 lb. honey (added to cooling wort)

1 oz. Fuggles hops

1 oz. of Juniper berries added to mash

Directions:

Bring 5 gallons of strike water to a boil with juniper branches and allow to cool. (Remove branches prior to mash) Juniper branches also added to first runnings and allowed to steep until the boil.

Single infusion mash at 155° for 60 minutes. Batch, sparge and flush with an additional 5 gallons at 175°.

60-minute boil with 1 ounce hops.

Add 1 pound honey to cooling wort.

When cooled to 70-75 degrees add S-33 yeast.

Primary fermentation: 2.5 Weeks

Secondary: 2.5 weeks

Bottle with 1 lb. corn sugar or keg

Snaps Song

(Melody: The Twelve
Days of Christmas)

For the first course of
Smorgasbord my hostess
gave to me...

A pickled herring and a cold beer

Two gravedlaks

Three shrimps on French bread

Four kinds of cold cuts

Five Aquavits . . . SKOAL!

Six frikadeller

Oh my head is swimming

Eight bites of cabbage

Nine pumpernickels

Ten types of cheeses

Eleven Danish cookies

Twelve cups of coffee

*Text by Mia Hansen,
Tucson, Arizona*

Norwegian Christmas Ale

Recipe by Scott Russell, printed in Brew Your Own magazine (December 1996)

Ingredients:

1 lb. crystal malt, 20° Lovibond (the # and degree tells you how much the malt has been roasted. At a lower degree the malt has a lighter caramel flavor; the higher the degree it has a more raisin flavor. Also can indicate the scale of color)

1 lb. crystal malt, 90° Lovibond

2 oz. roasted barley

7 lbs. amber malt extract syrup

4 oz. malto-dextrin powder

½ lb. light-brown sugar

1 oz. Chinook hop pellets

1 vanilla bean, chopped

1 tablespoon crushed cardamom seed

½ oz. Cascade hop flowers

Wyeast 1056 or 1272 (the numbers refer to the different strains of yeast)

¾ cup of dextrose for priming

Directions:

In 2.5 gallons of cold water, steep crystal malts and barley. Bring water gradually to 170° F and remove grains. Add to the kettle malt syrup, malto-dextrin powder, and sugar. Bring to a boil and add hops. Boil 45 minutes, then turn off heat. As the wort cools, steep hop flowers and, in a muslin bag, vanilla and cardamom. Cool, top up to 5.25 gallons, and pitch yeast. Ferment at 70° to 75° F for five to seven days. Rack to a secondary fermenter for a week. Prime and bottle.

Gløgg

Recipe from the Museum of Danish America

This festive punch is traditionally served with æbleskiver before Christmas and on other special occasions. Serve warm.

Ingredients:

6 cups cranberry-raspberry juice

1 cinnamon stick

6 whole cloves

½ tsp. cardamom, crushed

¼ cup sugar

½ cup raisins

¼ cup blanched whole almonds

Carlo Rossi burgundy wine (optional)

Directions:

Heat juice in a pot with spices. Bring it to a boil and then turn down the heat and let it simmer 10-15 minutes. Remove the cinnamon stick and the whole cloves. Add sugar, raisins, and almonds to the warm gløgg. When serving, be sure to get some raisins & almonds in the cups.

Do-It-Yourself Snaps

Ingredient Preparation Tips

 *Berries:* wash & leave whole, but score the skins on harder berries

 *Pineapple, mango & similar fruit:* wash & cut into chunks

 *Strawberries & citrus fruit:* wash & slice thinly or use zests of lemons & oranges

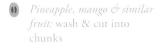 *Vanilla beans:* wash & cut lengthwise

 *Herbs:* wash & use whole (stems and all)

 *Peppers:* wash & leave whole or cut in half

Infused Aquavit

NOTE: to meet the criteria to be a true aquavit, it MUST have caraway. Anything else is called snaps.

Infusing spirits with flavor is a great way to experiment with your own personal tastes. The basic concept is to marry a variety of choice flavors into a base vodka to create a custom-flavored spirit. Choosing a good vodka that is smooth and clean will allow the added flavors to shine. Potato vodka is preferred for a Danish aquavit, but is not always accessible. Herbs, spices and fruits are most commonly used for infusions. The most popular infusions are fruit-based, however, you can use your imagination to create some wonderful combinations.

The Beginning:

The process itself is very easy. Choose a clean, air-tight jar: quart sized mason jars work well. Using smaller jars will allow you to divide a liter of vodka into a few jars, giving you the ability to create small batches of a variety of flavors at once. Wash the ingredients, place them inside the jar and fill it with vodka. Shake a few times and cover tightly with a lid. Shake daily for recommended time of infusion.

The Finish:

Once your infusion has reached its peak in flavor, you'll need to take the flavoring ingredients out of the jar. Use a fine strainer, cheesecloth or feed sack dishtowel to strain the vodka into another clean jar or bowl. You can return it to its original jar, if you would like, cleaning the jar thoroughly first. Store the finished infusion in the freezer.

General Infusion Times:

Use these times as a guideline for how long you should leave the ingredients in a jar of vodka – shaking several times daily.

1-2 hours: Hot peppers, though test it often as different peppers can flavor faster

3-4 days: Intense flavors such as basil, cucumber (3 days, skinless), dill, garlic, grapefruit, lemons, limes, mint, oranges, oregano, peppers, tarragon, thyme, and vanilla beans

7 days: Moderate flavors such as blackberries, blueberries, cantaloupes, lavender, mangoes, peaches, pitted cherries, raspberries, rosemary and strawberries (Infuse in refrigerator)

14 days: Mild flavors such as pineapple, ginger and lemongrass (Infuse in refrigerator)

Dild Aquavit.
Museum of Danish America

Dild Akvavit *(Dill aquavit)*

Recipe of Deb Christensen Larsen, Harlan, Iowa

Ingredients:

3 tsp. caraway seeds

3 tsp. sugar

3 large sprigs of fresh dill

3 oak chips

Splash of fine bourbon

Zesty Mint Aquavit

Recipe of Dennis Larson, Decorah, Iowa

Ingredients:

3 tsp. caraway seeds

3 tsp. fresh crushed mint leaves

3 tsp. orange zest

3 tsp. sugar

Walnut Snaps

Recipe of Lotte Hansen, Aalborg, Denmark

Directions:

Use the green nuts, which have to be plucked by August 15 (at least in Denmark). Wear gloves and cut the nuts in quarters. Cover them in vodka for a minimum 3 months, preferably 6. After filtering, thin the essence 1 part to 6 parts of clear vodka.

Faux Aalborg Jubilæums.
Museum of Danish America

Faux Aalborg Jubilæums *(Christmas aquavit)*

Recipe of Egon Bodtker, Salem, Oregon

Ingredients:

3 tsp. caraway seeds

1 tsp. coriander seeds

3 tsp. anise seeds

3 tsp. sugar

40 Snaps

Recipe of Lotte Hansen, Aalborg, Denmark

Ingredients:

40 tsp. sugar

40 coffee beans

1 orange, organic, prick 40 holes in it

2 vanilla pods

Directions:

Let it sit for 40 days.

Lime & Cumin Snaps

Recipe of Barb Larsen, Overland Park, Kansas

Ingredients:

¼ tsp. dry-roasted cumin seeds

Zest of one lime

Directions:

Roast cumin in dry skillet a couple of minutes. Shake pan to prevent burning.

When cool, put seeds and zest in with the vodka, recap, and allow to age for as long as your patience can wait (3 days is long enough).

Apple Pie Snaps.
Museum of Danish America

Apple Pie Snaps

Recipe of Deb Christensen Larsen, Harlan, Iowa

Ingredients:

2 apples, thinly sliced

6 tsp. sugar

3 cinnamon sticks

Sea Buckthorn Snaps

Recipe by Restaurant Kronborg, Copenhagen

Ingredients/Directions:

Place 1 ¼ cup of sea buckthorn in a bottle, fill the bottle with 1 pint of Brøndum clear snaps (Vodka is usable for a substitution), and add a tablespoon of liquid flower honey (preferably acacia honey). If you use fresh sea buckthorn, put them in your freezer for 24 hours before using.

Let the snaps infuse for 3-6 months in a dark and cold place (the refrigerator for instance); the longer the infusion time, the more prominent the flavor. Filter the snaps two to three times through a fine sieve or through a coffee filter before consumption. If you think the snaps is too sour you can add another two tablespoons of liquid honey.

Blackcurrant Snaps

Recipe by Restaurant Kronborg, Copenhagen

Ingredients/Directions:

Use 1 2/3 cups of fresh blackcurrants, washed and leaves picked, and mix with 7 oz. of sugar in a bottle. Then add a pint of Brøndum clear snaps (Vodka is usable for a substitution). Let the snaps infuse for a month in a dark and cold place (refrigerator will do). Shake the bottle a couple of times while the snaps is infusing to mix the sugar properly.

Filter the snaps through a fine sieve or through a coffee filter before consumption.

Cilantro Cucumber Snaps

Recipe of Lotte Hansen, Aalborg, Denmark

Ingredients:

1/3 large cucumber, cut into slices

1 small handful cilantro, cut

Directions:

Let the cucumbers steep for 4-5 days. Add the cilantro and steep another 1-2 days. Great with a Bloody Mary.

Snaps Song

(Melody: Lili Marlene)

You can give us herring

And you can give us sill

But you will still be erring

Unless you also will

Give us a glass of Akvavit

That sure smells sweet

To Swedes in heat

It gives the fish its feet

It makes the dish complete

Text by Christer Engström, from the Spritmuseum, Stockholm

Cilantro Cucumber Snaps.
Museum of Danish America

Cocktails

An Airplane *(En Flyver)*
Traditional Danish

This was especially popular in the early 20th century, when it was not socially acceptable for women to drink straight aquavit or beer.

Directions:

Mix aquavit with lemon sparkling water or lemon soda. Adjust to taste.

Coffee Punch also known as En Lille Sort *(A Little Black Cup)*
Traditional Danish

Directions:

Put a coin in your cup. Pour coffee in the cup until you can't see coin. Then pour aquavit until you can see coin again. Drink.

After Office Hours
Recipe from Arcus AS, Norway

An alternative to Irish Coffee

Ingredients:

2/3 oz. Grand Marnier Rouge

2/3 oz. Lysholm no 1 Aquavit

1/3 cup Strong black coffee

Heavy Cream

Mix everything but the cream and flavor with sugar if desired. Top with the cream and garnish with grated chocolate.

House Spirits Distillery began producing aquavit in 2007. The co-founder, Christian Krogstad, is Norwegian in heritage and grew up drinking aquavit. There were a lot of good aquavits being produced in the 2000s, but they weren't making their way to the United States, so he decided House Spirits Distillery should make their own.

Norwegian Wood

by Jeffery Morgenthaler, author of "The Bar Book: Elements of Cocktail Technique"

Ingredients:

1 oz. aquavit

1 oz. applejack

¾ oz. sweet vermouth

¼ oz. yellow Chartreuse

1 dash Angostura bitters

Stir ingredients with ice and strain into a chilled cocktail coupe. Garnish with a large twist of lemon peel.

Scandinavian Evening

Recipe by House Spirits Distillery

Ingredients:

1 ½ oz. Krogstad Festlig Aquavit

¼ oz. St. Elizabeth Allspice Dram

¾ oz. freshly squeezed lemon juice

½ oz. simple syrup

½ oz. club soda

Directions:

In a pint glass, add spirits and mixers (through simple syrup). Fill with ice and shake vigorously. Fine strain into an ice-filled collins glass and top with soda water. Garnish with a lemon wedge.

Scandinavian Evening.
House Spirits Distillery

Swedish 75.
American Swedish Institute

Swedish 75

Recipe from FIKA at the American Swedish Institute

Ingredients:

1 oz. dill aquavit

½ oz. lemon juice

½ oz. simple syrup

3 oz. sparkling wine

Lemon twist

Directions:

Combine first three ingredients in cocktail shaker with ice. Stir to incorporate. Strain into champagne flute. Top with sparkling wine. Garnish with lemon twist.

Course 3 Punch

Recipe from Gamle Ode

(Serves 4)

Ingredients:

7 oz. Gamle Ode Celebration Aquavit

1 oz. Kronan Swedish Punsch

2 oz. grapefruit juice

2 oz. fresh lemon juice

2 oz. simple syrup

¼ oz. Bittercube Jamaican #2 Bitters

8-10 oz. seltzer

Cherries

Grated nutmeg

Directions:

Stir all ingredients, including seltzer, together in a 4-cup measuring vessel. Pour into a punch bowl and add one large piece of ice. Serve in glasses with one ice cube and a cherry, then grate nutmeg over the top.

"Why Gamle Ode? This "old ode" is my way of honoring the people who introduced me to aquavit and smørrebrød, and my general debt of gratitude to all Scandinavians—from Iceland to Denmark, with touches of Sweden, Finland, and Norway. Gamle Ode is an ode in part to the actual beverage, but also to the cultural experience and the richness of celebration with family and friends who share these aquavit occasions. In short, to the heartfelt moment that accompanies the word: Skål, Skál, Kippis, Skol, Skaal, Skal, Cheers!"

Mike, founder of Gamle Ode

Fresh dill is a critical ingredient for Gamle Ode Dill Aquavit.
Photo by Kimberly Ann Newman and Mike McCarron

Dill Martini

Recipe from Gamle Ode

Ingredients:

1 ½ oz. Gamle Ode Dill Aquavit

½ oz. gin

¾ oz. Cocchi Vermouth di Torino (sweet vermouth)

¼ oz. Dolin Dry Vermouth

1 dropper Bittercube Orange Bitters

Lemon twist

Fresh dill sprig

Directions:

Stir ingredients over ice and strain into a martini glass. Garnish with a lemon twist and sprig of dill.

Linie Cranberry

Recipe from Arcus AS, Norway

Ingredients:

1 ½ oz. Linie Aquavit

¾ oz. lime syrup

Cranberry juice

Directions:

Combine aquavit and lime syrup in an ice-filled collins glass. Fill up with cranberry juice.

Norwegian Blonde.
Old Ballard Liquor Company

Norwegian Blonde

Recipe from Old Ballard Liquor Co.

Ingredients:

Juice of ½ lemon + simple syrup to taste (or good-quality lemonade) to equal 4 oz.

4 large springs fresh dill, chopped roughly

2 oz. Riktig Caraway Aquavit

Directions:

Add all ingredients to a shaker with ice, and shake HARD. Strain into a glass and serve with a garnish of fresh dill sprig.

Knotty Viking.
Photo by pinkpatisserie.net

Knotty Viking

Recipe from Old Ballard Liquor Co.

Ingredients:

2 oz. Riktig Caraway Aquavit

Lime wedge

Splash simple syrup

Dry Cucumber Soda

Cucumber slice (for garnish)

Directions:

Muddle the lime, aquavit and simple syrup with ice. Top
with Dry Cucumber Soda and garnish with a cucumber slice.

Oysters and Aquavit

Älskar Aquavit Oyster Mignonette

Recipe from Old Ballard Liquor Co.

Ingredients:

1 1/2 oz. Älskar Citron Aquavit

1/2 oz. white vinegar

1 tbs. finely-diced shallot

2 tsp. freshly-ground black pepper

Directions:

Mix and drizzle over freshly-shucked oysters on the half shell.

Aquavit Oyster Shooters

Recipe from Old Ballard Liquor Co.

Directions:

Place one raw oyster into a shotglass or cordial glass. Pour in Älskar Citron
Aquavit to cover the oyster. Grate fresh horseradish root on top to equal ¼ tsp.
Garnish with a lemon wedge.

Scandinavian-Inspired Dishes

Danish-American Rye Bread

Recipe by Marianne Frøsig Sørensen, Fredericia, Denmark

Ingredients:

2 bottles of beer, Pilsner or darker (you can experiment with the flavors)

1 cup water

1 tablespoon yeast

5 cups rye flour

1 cup sunflower seeds

¾ cup flax seeds

1 teaspoon salt

Directions:

Mix beer, water and yeast in a bowl. Make sure that the liquid is a little warmer than room temperature. Add the seeds, flax, flour and salt. Mix it together and make sure that there are no lumps of flour in the bottom of the bowl. Let it rise for 2 hours.

Divide the dough in half and place each in a well-greased loaf pan. Let it rise for another 1½-2 hours.

Take a fork and stab the dough carefully a couple of times before placing it in the preheated 410° F oven for 1 – 1 ¼ hour.

Take the bread out of the oven. Remove from the pan; you may have to use a knife around the edge of the loaf pan to loosen the bread. Wrap the bread in a damp tea towel and let it cool on a rack. When cooled off, place the bread in a plastic bag and let it sit for one day before you slice it.

Lefse Chips and Lingonberry Salsa

Recipe by Patrice Johnson, http://culturalconstruct.blogspot.com/, Twin Cities, Minnesota

Crisped lefse makes a delicious and unique chip for dipping.

Serving suggestion: light lager-style beer

For the chips: Slice lefse rounds into smaller sections; coat both sides with non-stick spray. Place chips in single layers on baking sheet and bake at 325 degrees until chips just begin to crisp, flipping after 3 minutes. Be careful that lefse doesn't burn.

For the lingonberry salsa: combine equal parts of your favorite salsa (add a squeeze of lime and handful of cilantro if using jarred) with lingonberry preserves.

Apple pork / *Æbleflæsk.*
Photo by Thomas Alcayaga,
www.madetmere.dk, Copenhagen

Apple Pork / *Æbleflæsk*, a Classic with a Twist

Recipe and photo by Thomas Alcayaga, www.madetmere.dk, Copenhagen.
Translated by Johannes Kristoffersen

Serves two for dinner. Serves more if part of lunch. The dish might seem confusing, but it is not that complicated. The dish takes around 30 to 40 minutes to prepare, which basically is the time the pork needs in the oven.

Ingredients:

Pickled onions

5-6 shallots

½ cup vinegar

½ cup sugar

½ cup water

Spices: bay leaves, fennel seeds, star anise and peppercorns

Apples

5 apples

½ cup apple juice (or water)

2 tablespoons brown sugar

2 tablespoons apple cider vinegar

A little cooking fat

Salt and pepper

Soft Onions

7 oz. onions

Cooking fat (I used duck fat, but bacon fat or butter will do)

In addition

14 oz pork loin

Rye bread

Directions:

Begin by putting the pork loin in a baking pan. Put some baking parchment beneath it. Season with some salt and pepper. Preheat the oven to 350 degrees. Roast it for 30 to 40 minutes.

Then to the pickled onions: Put vinegar, sugar and water in a pot. Season with your favorite spices. My favorites are listed in the ingredients, but you can also use mustard seeds and coriander seeds. The spices I use give a sort of licorice- like, taste which I like in combination with the different elements of the dish. Bring contents to a boil and make sure the sugar is melted. Cut the shallots lengthwise and roast them on a dry pan till they are slightly brown. Add them to the pot, remove it from the stove and let it steep until you serve the dish.

Now on to the apples: Ready a pan with a little duck fat (or butter, oil, or bacon fat). Fry the apples, which should be cut in cubes without the core. Roast them for 5 minutes and add the apple juice. I like my apples boiled out, so I add the liquid. Add the brown sugar and let it bubble. Flavor with apple cider vinegar, salt and pepper. Flavor till you find the right balance, it all depends on the apples.

For the soft onions, you just cut the onions into rings. Then you fry them in plenty of cooking fat. After the initial heating you turn down the heat and let them caramelize.

When the pork is done all you have to do is serve the dish! Rye bread topped with the apple then pork, soft onions and pickled onions. I like to serve the dish with a dark beer or a snaps/aquavit.

Danish Meatballs / *Frikadeller*

Recipe by Marianne Frøsig Sørensen, Fredericia, Denmark

Ingredients:

1 lb. ground pork

1 lb. ground beef

1 onion finely chopped

2 eggs

2-3 tablespoons flour

2-3 tablespoons oatmeal

½ cup milk

1 teaspoon salt

Ground nutmeg

Ground pepper

Directions:

Mix all the ingredients in a big bowl. Let it rest for 10-15 minutes. Shape the meatballs with a tablespoon in your hand and fry them in a skillet, in melted butter at medium heat. When starting to turn grey, turn the meatball over and fry it on the other side. Turn the meatballs a couple of times until cooked all the way through.

Fish Balls with Salmon /
Fiskefrikadeller med Laks

Recipe and photo by Restaurant Kronborg,
http://www.restaurantkronborg.dk, Copenhagen.

Fish balls with remoulade is a classic Danish *smørrebrød* – and always a popular lunch dish with our guests, young as old. We hope you enjoy the recipe.

Fish Balls.
Restaurant Kronborg,
www.restaurantkronborg.dk

Ingredients:

2 lbs. of fish (½ salmon, ½ pollock)

3 eggs

1 pepper, chopped finely (brunoise)

½ bunch of chives, chopped finely

½ yellow onion, chopped coarsely

1 pint of heavy cream

Spices:

Juice of one freshly-squeezed lemon

1 ½ teaspoon salt

½ teaspoon black pepper

Relish:

Remoulade, *(see recipe for homemade Remoulade on the next page)*

Garnish:

Lemon wedges

Fresh dill

Canola oil

Rye bread and butter

Directions:

Blend fish and salt. Add eggs, onions, lemon juice and pepper. Finally add heavy cream and blend till the mass is blank and firm.

Mix chives and peppers in the finished mince and add extra salt, pepper and lemon juice to your liking.

Make fish balls in the size of a large hen's egg with a two metal spoons and fry the fish balls in oil on a pan at medium heat until they are dark golden (3-4 minutes on each side).

Arrange the hot fish balls on a platter or portion them on plates.

Garnish with a sizeable dollop of remoulade, lemon wedges, and the fresh dill.

Serve with sliced rye bread and butter.

Tip:

If you have some left-over smoked salmon, you can replace up to 1/5 of the fish with the smoked salmon. It gives the fish balls a more smoky and intense flavor.

Drink:

We recommend a fresh, light beer for the fish balls, like Böhmer Pilsner or New York Lager from Nørrebro Bryghus, and a fresh dill aquavit or a tangier aquavit, like the chili lemon aquavit from Schumachers or our own home-made Sea Buckthorn Snaps *(recipe on page 72)*.

Remoulade, the Favorite Relish of the Danes

Recipe and photo by Restaurant Kronborg,
http://www.restaurantkronborg.dk/,Copenhagen.

For a Dane, remoulade is the perfect relish for classic *smørrebrød* (open-faced sandwich), like pan-fried fish fillets, Danish fish balls or roast beef with crisp onions.

Remoulade,
Restaurant Kronborg,
www.restaurantkronborg.dk

Ingredients:

1 pint of sweet pickles

½ cup mayonnaise, preferably home-made

½ cup capers, extra fine

Salt and pepper

Directions:

Blend the pickles till they have the consistency you prefer (we prefer ours rather coarse).

Add mayonnaise and capers and adjust the flavor with salt and pepper.

Aquavit Sandwich.
Restaurant Kronborg,
www.restaurantkronborg.dk,
Photo by Chris Tonnesen

Aquavit Sandwich –
Potato Sandwich with Chive Crème

Recipe and picture by Restaurant Kronborg,
http://www.restaurantkronborg.dk/, Copenhagen.
Photo by Chris Tonnesen

We make our version of the popular 'aquavit sandwich' with old-fashioned marinated herrings and chive crème – of course it tastes even better with new Danish potatoes.

Makes 10 open-faced sandwiches.

The 'aquavit sandwich' did not get its name because it is made with aquavit but because it tastes great with it...

Ingredients:

2.2 lb. new potatoes

10 slices of rye bread

6-8 fillets of old-fashioned marinated herring, sliced into thin strips or cut into cubes (approx. 0.1 lb. of herring per sandwich)

Chive crème:

1 bunch fresh chives

¾ to 1 cup sour cream

¾ to 1 cup mayonnaise (preferably home-made)

Juice from one lemon

Salt and pepper to taste

Garnish:

½ bunch of chives, finely chopped

½ cup deep-fried capers

Directions:

Boil the potatoes till tender. Leave to cool and slice.

Wash the chives and pat them dry. Chop the chives finely and mix them with lemon juice, sour cream and mayonnaise. Add salt and pepper to taste.

Butter the bread and layer the sliced potatoes on top. Arrange the chive crème and herring fillets on top of the potatoes. Garnish with chives and deep-fried capers.

Alternative:

If you mix the herring cubes with the chive crème you get what the Swedes call "gubbröra" (or "Old man's mix"), which tastes great when topped on cold boiled potatoes – or as spread on dark rye bread.

 *Æbleskiver*

Recipe by Marianne Frøsig Sørensen, Fredericia, Denmark

Should yield approximately 50.

Ingredients:

4 jumbo or 5 large eggs

2 cups milk or buttermilk

½ tablespoon melted butter

2 ¼ cups plain flour

2 tablespoon sugar

4 teaspoons baking powder

If you are in a festive mood you can add the following: a pinch of cardamom (about a ¼ tsp) and finely grated lemon zest.

Directions:

Separate the eggs. Whisk the yolks, milk, and melted butter together in a mixing bowl; add the flour, spices, and baking powder. Whisk the egg whites and carefully fold them in to the batter.

The fun part: Bake'em… When warm, add a little bit of butter to each of the little cups in the pan. We normally use salted butter in the æbleskiver pan but you can also use oil. Heat the pan, on medium heat. Pour in about 2 tablespoons of batter, so it levels close to the top edge of the cup. As soon as they get bubbly around the edge, turn them halfway, so that the baked crust is standing vertically in the cup. After a while you turn them the remaining 90°. This will give them a perfect ball-shape. Use a knitting needle or a fork for the turning. Continue cooking, turning the ball to keep it from burning.

Serve them with a side of raspberry jam and powdered sugar for dunking.

They will keep in the fridge for up to 2 days. You can freeze them (not for longer than 3 months) and reheat in the oven (10-15 minutes at 250 F), but they will not taste as good as fresh baked.

Savory *Æbleskiver.*

Photo by Patrice Johnson,
calledtothetable.blogspot.com,
Twin Cities, Minnesota

Savory Herb-Cheese *Æbleskiver*

Recipe by Patrice Johnson, http://culturalconstruct.blogspot.com/,
Twin Cities, Minnesota

Makes about 20 æbleskiver

Pairing suggestion: bock- or lager-style beer

Ingredients:

1 ½ cups flour

½ teaspoon baking powder

1 teaspoon baking soda

¼ teaspoon salt

1 cup sour or buttermilk

2 eggs, beaten

1 cup sour cream or yogurt

3 tablespoons fresh chives, dill, basil, and parsley; chopped
very fine (use a single herb or combine for more flavor)

4 ounces (about ½ cup) Gruyère cheese, sliced into 20 small cubes

Vegetable oil for frying

Directions:

In large mixing bowl sift together flour, baking powder, baking soda, and salt.
In small mixing bowl whisk together buttermilk, eggs, sour cream or yogurt,
and herbs. Stir wet ingredients into dry and set batter aside for 5 to 10 minutes.

Heat æbleskiver pan over medium-high heat. Add 1/2 teaspoon vegetable oil
to each pancake well. Fill wells 2/3 full with batter. Gently push one cube
of cheese into the middle of each cake round. Turn with fork (or skewer, or
chopstick) when cakes are brown on the bottom: loosen top edges with
skewers, turning 1/4 around when pancakes starts to bubble. Turn again 4
times or until golden orb forms and inside of pancake is cooked thoroughly.

Serve with butter, a fresh grating of cheese, and chopped herbs.

Scandinavian Spring Beer Cheese Soup

Recipe by Patrice Johnson, http://culturalconstruct.blogspot.com/,
Twin Cities, Minnesota

4 generous servings

Paring suggestion: lager or ale-style beer used in making soup

Scandinavian Spring Beer Cheese Soup.
Photo by Patrice Johnson,
calledtothetable.blogspot.com,
Twin Cities, Minnesota

Ingredients:

2 tablespoons butter

½ yellow onion, diced

1 celery stalk, diced

1 carrot, diced

¼ cup red or yellow pepper, diced

2 cloves garlic, smashed

1 teaspoon each prepared mustard, paprika, Worcestershire sauce

2 tablespoons flour

12 ounces lager or ale-style beer

2 cups chicken broth

1 potato, peeled and diced

3 ounces cream cheese

¼ cup sour cream

1 cup shredded Jarslberg or Swiss cheese

½ cup shredded Emmenthal or Gruyère cheese

½ cup cream or half-n-half (optional)

Zest from one orange

¼ teaspoon nutmeg

Directions:

In large stockpot sauté onion, celery, carrot, and pepper in butter until soft, about 5 minutes; season to taste with salt and black pepper. Add garlic and whisk in mustard, paprika, Worcestershire, and flour and continue whisking over medium heat about 1 minute. Increase heat and add beer, broth, and potato; bring to low simmer and cook uncovered 15 minutes.

Use an immersion blender or process in batches to puree vegetables. Over medium heat add cream cheese, sour cream, and shredded cheeses to soup and stir until cheeses are melted and well incorporated. Stir in cream if desired.

Season soup with orange zest and nutmeg; serve with Rye Pretzel Bites with Caraway *(recipe on page 90).*

Grilled Biff à la Lindström Sliders

Recipe by Patrice Johnson, http://culturalconstruct.blogspot.com/, Twin Cities, Minnesota

Makes 8 small patties

Pairing suggestion: pale ale or wheat-style beer

Grilled Biff à la Lindström Sliders.
*Photo by Patrice Johnson,
calledtothetable.blogspot.com,
Twin Cities, Minnesota*

Ingredients:

1 lb. ground beef

1 small white onion, grated

¼ cup cooked potatoes, riced and cooled

¼ cup pickled beet, diced

1 tablespoon capers, diced

1 tablespoon prepared mustard

2 egg yolks

Salt and pepper to taste

Directions:

Combine all ingredients and form into 8 small patties. Grill over medium heat until cooked medium well.

Serve sliders on onion buns (if buns are large, cut them into quarters) with pickled beets and cucumbers, or mustard and a dab of lingonberry preserves.

Alternatively: serve burgers with grilled flatbread or lefse and top with a salad of yogurt, cucumber, and dill.

Cured Game

Recipe by Arcus AS, Norway

By "game" Norwegians usually mean elk or reindeer, but any game will do. A less "wild," but extremely tasty version can be made from beef. The following recipe is sufficient for six portions.

Ingredients:

2 lbs. sirloin steak of wild game or beef

3 tablespoons salt

3 tablespoons sugar

1 teaspoon coarsely ground pepper

2 teaspoons dried thyme/sweet basil

¾ cup Linie Aquavit

Directions:

Cut away the tendons, membranes and fat from the meat. Rub in a mixture of salt, sugar and herbs. Place the meat in a dish and pour the aquavit over. Cover with foil and leave 4 – 5 days in the fridge. Turn the meat daily. Remove the herbs. Cut the meat in thin slices prior to serving.

Gravlax Pizza

Recipe by Patrice Johnson, http://culturalconstruct.blogspot.com/,
Twin Cities, Minnesota

One lefse round serves 2 to 4

Serving suggestion: aquavit, any style, especially if used in the gravlax cure

Gravlax Pizza.
Photo by Patrice Johnson.
calledtothetable.blogspot.com.
Twin Cities, Minnesota

Ingredients:

1 large lefse round

3 tablespoons whole-fat Greek-style yogurt

3 tablespoons sour cream

2 to 3 ounces gravlax, sliced thin (see recipe below)

Pickled cucumbers

Red onions, sliced thin

Capers, caviar, fresh dill and chives

Olive oil

Directions:

Brush a generous amount of olive oil on each side of lefse round. Place on baking sheet and bake in 325-degree oven on both sides until just crisp but do not burn; about 10 minutes.

In small bowl whisk together yogurt and sour cream.

Remove lefse from oven and spread yogurt/sour cream mixture over top. Dot with salmon, cucumbers, onion, capers, caviar, dill and chives. Slice and serve immediately.

For the gravlax (ingredients):

1 lb. sushi-grade salmon, skin on

1/2 cup sugar

1/4 cup salt

1 teaspoon fresh cracked pepper

6 to 8 sprigs fresh dill, stems attached

1/2 shot dill flavored aquavit such as Gamle Ode
(or juniper infused vodka or gin)

For the gravlax (directions):

Slice the salmon into two uniform halves.

Place one salmon fillet skin-side down on large sheet of plastic wrap. Combine dry ingredients and rub half into salmon on both sides. Layer dill over flesh and spritz with half of the aquavit. Do the same for the other fillet, then plank second fillet, skin-side up, over first fillet. Rub remaining cure over second fillet. Wrap plastic around fish, pressing together. Lay in glass dish at room temperature 4 hours. Refrigerate salmon additional 36 hours, flipping fish every 12 hours. The cure will liquefy during curing process.

Remove plastic and cure; rinse fish and pat dry with paper towels. Slice paper thin.

Rye Pretzel Bites with Caraway.

Photo by Patrice Johnson,
calledtothetable.blogspot.com,
Twin Cities, Minnesota

Rye Pretzel Bites with Caraway

Recipe by Patrice Johnson, http://culturalconstruct.blogspot.com/,
Twin Cities, Minnesota

Makes 24

Ingredients:

½ cup baking soda

3 cups all-purpose flour

1 cup rye flour

1 package instant yeast (about 2 ¼ teaspoons)

3 tablespoons brown sugar, plus 1 ½ tablespoons brown sugar for bath

1 teaspoon caraway seeds

½ teaspoon salt

Zest and juice from 1 orange, separated

2 tablespoons butter, room temp

1 cup warm water

1 egg yolk

2 to 3 teaspoons each caraway seeds and coarse salt,
mixed together in small bowl

Directions:

Preheat oven to 250 degrees. Pour baking soda on parchment lined baking sheet and bake for 30 minutes. Remove from oven and cool.

In large mixing bowl combine flour, rye, yeast, 3 tablespoons of the brown sugar, caraway, salt, and orange zest. Use hands to blend butter into flour as evenly as you can. Add water and stir until dough comes together. Remove from bowl and knead 10 to 15 minutes or until smooth. Shape into a ball and return to bowl; cover with plastic wrap or clean kitchen towel and let rise in warm place until doubled, 1 to 2 hours.

Gently remove dough from bowl and divide into 24 pieces. Shape into bite-sized twig or round. Place bites on well-oiled parchment lined baking sheets. Cover sheets with clean kitchen towel and let rest 30 minutes.

Preheat oven to 425 degrees; place racks on bottom and upper thirds of oven.

Bring 2 ½ quarts (10 cups) of water to boil and add baking soda and 1 ½ tablespoons brown sugar. Stir to dissolve and reduce heat to simmer.

Gently place a few pretzel bites at a time in simmering bath. Turn after 30 second and simmer additional 30 seconds. Remove bites with a slotted spoon or spider and return to prepared parchment. Continue simmering bites in batches.

In small mixing bowl whisk together egg yolk and 1 to 2 tablespoons orange juice. Brush tops of pretzel bites with yolk mixture. Sprinkle tops with caraway-salt mixture.

Bake 5 to 7 minutes, and then switch rack positions; bake additional 5 minutes or until pretzels are dark and crisp on the outside. Serve hot.

Aquavit Sherbet
Recipe by Arcus AS, Norway

Neither lemon nor sherbet belong to traditional Norwegian cuisine. The following combination proves, however, that aquavit is versatile and perfectly suited to exotic fruits and modern flavors.

Ingredients:

2 cups water

1 ¼ cups sugar

Rind of one lemon

Juice of ½ lemon

½ cup Linie Aquavit

2 egg whites

Directions:

Remove the lemon rind with a potato peeler. Boil sugar, water and the rind for about five minutes. Add the lemon juice, allow to cool and then strain. Add aquavit to the syrup according to taste, and freeze until it has the consistency of a sherbet. Stir from time to time during the freezing process. Beat the egg-whites until stiff and mix with the sherbet. Return to freezer until completely frozen. Serve in individual dishes and garnish with thin twists of lemon peel or toasted almonds.

Recipes Index